Zoglin, Mary Lou

Power and politi-
cs in the commu-
nity college

# the Community College

## Mary Lou Zoglin

1976

# C P

*Library of Congress Cataloging in Publication Data*

Zoglin, Mary Lou, 1928–
   Power and politics in the community college.

   Bibliography: p.
   Includes index.
   1.  Community colleges – United States – History.
   2.  Community colleges – United States – Administration.
     I. Title.
   LB2328.Z63     378'.052'0973          75–35618

   ISBN 0–88280–037–X

Copyright © 1976 by ETC PUBLICATIONS
Palm Springs
California 92262

TO

Z

# Table
# of
# Contents

# Foreword
# by
# Joseph P. Cosand

An analysis of power and politics in the community college has been needed for the past quarter of a century. As the rapid expansion of these institutions began in the 1950's, there was a mesmerization with growth, but little attention was paid to the changing roles of internal and external power groups, and to the politics being employed by these power groups. In retrospect, it was an age of innocence similar to what used to be believed about our adolescent children. The community colleges were in their adolescence. They were growing rapidly, were awkward and ungainly, were insecure in their rapid growth, were too often defensive in their new role as a participating and integral part of higher education.

The dominance of school superintendents and public school boards, which controlled the appendage-like junior colleges, was being challenged in the local communities, in the state capitals, and certainly in the colleges. These challenges resulted in a gradual separation, institution by institution and state by state, of the junior college from the high school and in the formation of community college districts. The community colleges thus entered the age of youthful maturity with the accompanying problems of defensiveness and arrogance. These confrontive actions were viewed by collegiate and university power groups with suspicion, disdain, and tolerance, and by legislative and executive groups with support and hope for a new day in higher education – separate and apart from the traditional four-year college and university.

Ms. Zoglin brings to the reader a most perceptive viewpoint and understanding of the community college, its role in the community, and power loci and politics involved in the development and evolution of this unique American institution. No segment escapes her attention. The lay citizen, board, president, administrative staff, faculty, support staff, and students are discussed as role players in power and political adventures. So also, are the local and state politicians explored with projections made concerning the future roles of the state executive and legislative branches of government.

The warnings are made with respect to the tenuousness of continued local community college autonomy, as the author reflects upon the inroads made by the state and the federal governments into the power and politics of the community colleges.

Community college leaders, board members, and professionals have gradually become aware of their role in the power plays within higher education and of the politics within and supportive of such power plays. In some areas of the country, both locally and statewide, this awareness has been too little and too late. In other areas, it is touch-and-go, and in still others there is time to act to prevent a takeover by a state office or by a "senior" institution of this maturing young giant in postsecondary education.

Ms. Zoglin, with her rich experience as a community college board member and now as a state board member for community colleges, tells the story well. Reality prevents us from closing our eyes to power and politics, no matter how some professional educators recoil at such awareness, acceptance and involvement. Reality then demands that the community colleges assume their leadership role cooperatively with other institutions of higher education, locally, statewide, and regionally. Without such reality and cooperative planning, state or regional planning initiated and administered by power groups external to the colleges themselves will assume the prerogatives of planning for, and administration of postsecondary education in some or all of its parts.

# Preface

The community college is the fastest growing segment of American education today. Its potential for touching the lives of citizens of all ages and in all walks of life appears almost limitless. As the youngest and least tradition-bound of our educational institutions, its future course is still open. Thus citizens, students, and staff all have an interest in learning how to influence the evolution of "their" community colleges.

The governance structure of the community college bears a surface resemblance to that of other educational institutions. Its boards of trustees are like those in the public school system, its academic senates like those in four-year colleges, and its relations with legislative bodies and higher education agencies like those of the state universities. In reality, however, community colleges have done more than simply borrow certain characteristics from other members of the school family; they are modifying them to form a governance structure of their own that will enable them to perform their special mission in society.

Even those most intimately involved with the community colleges usually do not understand this system. Their efforts to effect change are therefore often misdirected, leading to feelings of futility and frustration. In order to be effective, they must be aware of the role of all the interested parties and of the relationship among them. They need to know how much authority each group — the federal government, the state legislatures and their regulatory agencies, local citizens, trustees, students, faculty, and administrators — possesses and why it has been so allocated.

Information is readily available on many of the factors that enter into the decision-making process. The growing power of faculty, the desirability of student involvement, the waning authority of college presidents, the expansion of state and federal controls, and the ways by which citizens influence educational institutions — all are discussed in existing books and articles. But nowhere has the effort been made to relate all of these factors, to explain how they mesh to form the governance structure of today's community colleges.

In *Power and Politics in the Community College* I try to show how decisions are actually made by describing the role of all participant groups and explaining their interaction. Further illustration of this process is provided by fictional case studies of specific policy-making incidents in different types of community colleges. Although none of these incidents took place exactly as described in any one community college, all of the elements are drawn from real-life situations. My hope is that with *Power and Politics in the Community College* as a guide to the general topography of governance, interested parties will be able to analyse the decision-making structure and process in their own community colleges and move effectively to influence them.

I am most grateful to the many people who have helped me in this endeavor. In particular, my thanks go to Robert Lombardi, Lorraine Anderson, John Dunn, Elizabeth Martin, William Meardy, A. Robert DeHart, Lloyd Messersmith, JoAnne Martz, Elaine Felder, Iris Swanson, John Lombardi, John Tirrell, Ervin Harlacher, Joseph Cosand, and William Tinsley, who supplied encouragement and practical assistance along the way.

# CHAPTER 1
# The Present's Debt
# to the Past

The community college has been called an institution without a past. Due to its extreme youth, so the story goes, it is unfettered by the traditions that so constrain its sister institutions of higher education. It alone is still free to chart its own course, to develop independently of the heavy hand of history.

This picture is, unfortunately, not completely accurate. It is true that the community college is a mere babe in arms when compared to other colleges and universities. While their origins date back many centuries, the community college was not even a gleam in anyone's eye until the late 1800's. This does not mean, however, that it has been untouched by events that took place before that time. Its destiny — like that of human beings — was to a great extent predetermined at birth by its parents and its cultural heritage. Thus, a look at its family tree and at the traditions inherited from its predecessors will go far towards explaining the community college of today.

### Ancestry

In retrospect, the emergence of the community college in twentieth century America seems inevitable. It all began in the 1640's when the Puritan settlers established compulsory, tax-supported schools. From then on the public school system expanded steadily in response to an apparently insatiable demand for learning on the part of the American public. By 1850 free elementary education for all children was the rule; secondary education, however, remained the province of the private academies. As the number of elementary graduates grew, so did the pressure to provide additional schooling at public expense. Boston had a public high school as early as 1821; several hundred were in existence by the time of the Civil War. The right of local boards of education to maintain free high schools and support them with public funds was affirmed by the landmark Kalamazoo case in 1874, thus clearing away the last legal obstacle to public secondary education. After that, growth was rapid: enrollment spurted from 72,000 in 1870 to 519,000 in 1900,[1] with the number of graduates increasing from 16,000 to 95,000 in that same period.[2] It was now a question of when — not if — community colleges would be added to the system. Sooner or later, these high school graduates were going to insist that higher education too be made available to them.

If the title of "mother" of the community colleges rightfully belongs to the public school system, that of "father" must surely go to the state universities. The existence of a long-standing tradition of state-supported higher education — dating back to colonial times — was of immeasurable help to the emerging community colleges. The University of North Carolina, for example, was provided for in the state constitution of 1776 and opened in 1795. Interestingly, several states first tried to provide public higher education the easy way, by simply taking over such existing private colleges as Yale, Columbia, and Harvard. When they were stymied in this effort by the Supreme Court decision in the Dartmouth College case of 1819, they turned to establishing their own universities. The Indiana constitution of 1816 made it the duty of the general assembly "to provide by law for a general system of education, ascending in a regular gradation from township schools to a state university, wherein tuition shall be gratis, and equally open to all."[3]

By the time of the Civil War, the desirability of tax-supported, state-controlled higher education was widely accepted, with 20 such institutions in operation. Their future was assured by the passage in 1862 of the federal Morrill Act, which gave substantial land grants to the states for agricultural and mechanical colleges. With this financial stimulus, the state university movement expanded rapidly during the latter half of the nineteenth century.

This was part of a national trend which saw enrollment in all of higher education — private as well as public — jump from 52,000 in 1870 to 157,000 in 1890 and to 238,000 in 1900.[4]

## Birth

Not everyone, however, was happy about the burgeoning demand for higher education. Some of the most prestigious university educators of the day were afraid that their institutions would be inundated by the rising tide of applicants. Accustomed as we are to counting each year's graduating class in the millions, the 95,000 young people completing high school in 1900 hardly seem cause for alarm. But to the educators of the turn of the century, it apparently seemed that the barbarian hordes were about to descend on the sacred Halls of Academe. Instead of opening their doors wider to accommodate them, they proposed to close them to all freshmen and sophomores. This was in frank imitation of the German university system, which had long been greatly admired by a group of top American educators. By relegating lower division work to some other institution, they hoped to halt the feared deterioration of the university and to free it to concentrate on its "real" tasks of specialized instruction and research.

The leaders of this movement were men like Henry P. Tappan of the University of Michigan, Alexis F. Lange of the University of California, William W. Folwell of Illinois, Richard H. Jesse of Missouri, David Starr Jordan of Stanford, and — probably the most important of all — William Rainey Harper of the University of Chicago.[5] Their primary goal was to upgrade the American university by moving it in the direction of the German model. They were, at the same time, sincerely interested in making post-secondary education available to more young people. Since these goals seem to be contradictory, to attempt to achieve them both at the same time appears ridiculous. But the Gods must have smiled on their endeavors, for they led them to the one institution that could conceivably solve their problem: the community college.

Although there is disagreement as to where the first public community college was established (Greeley, Colorado, in the 1880's? Saginaw, Michigan, in 1895? Joliet, Illinois, in 1901?), the idea was certainly in the air at that time.[6] And what better way to do everything they had in mind than through a nation-wide network of public two-year colleges! They would put post-high school education within reach of many more students; they would relieve the pressure on the universities to accept ever more freshmen; and they might even lead to the hoped-for elimination of all lower division work from the universities.

Thus did the elitist forces seeking to close the universities to the masses and the democratic forces seeking to open higher education to them join together to promote the community colleges. And promote them they did! Harper *et al* set about helping found community colleges, guaranteeing the transfer-ability of their courses, spreading the word about their advantages, and even persuading state legislatures to pass laws encouraging their growth. The long-term effect of all this activity is difficult to assess, but they did provide intellectual respectability, publi-city, and practical help to the fledgling institutions. At the very least, their contributions were those of the midwife: they used their skills to hasten and make easier the birth of the community colleges.

### Adolescence

Small wonder, then, that the community colleges experienced a major identity crisis during their early years. Each group of back-ers tried to foist a different role model on the young institutions: some wanted them to emulate the German *gymnasia* so that Stanford or Michigan might become a second Heidelberg; others hoped they would continue the public school philosophy of offer-ing varying programs for students of varying abilities; and still others expected the junior colleges — as they were called then — to be just what their name implied: a truncated version of a four-year institution.

This profusion of prototypes led to a great deal of confusion within the community college movement. It was responsible for the tremendous amount of time spent on the great debate over the "true nature" of the community college. At times it seemed that schizophrenia was imminent, with some institutions demand-ing to be classified as higher education and others arguing with equal vehemence for retaining the secondary designation. Naturally, many played both sides against the middle, choosing to stand with the high schools when that route promised greater financial security and with the universities when considerations of prestige were paramount.

As the community colleges grew in size and in public acceptance, they outgrew their identity crisis and emerged into adulthood with a real feeling of self-worth. No longer content to be merely an appendage of some other level of education, they are proud of their status as a new and unique social institution. While acknowledging a debt to both secondary and higher education, they no longer feel the need to be identified as anything other than community colleges.

### Governance

Their new-found independence has enabled the colleges to break away from many of the traditions inherited from their educational forebears. In the field of governance, however, community college practices continue to resemble those developed at other levels of the educational system. Before looking at these, a brief digression seems in order: what does the word "governance" really mean?

The massive Oxford English Dictionary, although it devotes 146 lines to "governance" and traces its origin back to the 14th century, does not include a definition even remotely applicable to an educational institution. The American Heritage Dictionary comes somewhat closer: it describes "governance" as meaning "to make and administer public policy for a political unit."[7] Other dictionaries and encyclopedias take a similar approach: either they do not define it at all or they assign to it a meaning much too general for our purposes.

Most writers on this topic seem to share with *Alice in Wonderland's* Humpty Dumpty the feeling that "When I use a word, it means just what I choose it to mean — neither more nor less."[8] Some, for example, include in their definition only the internal organizational structure of the college — the mechanism by which teachers, administrators, students, and trustees collaborate in decision-making; others think of it in terms of the governing board alone; and still others take it to mean the external superstructure which sits on top of each individual college - state boards of education, coordinating councils, vocational advisory committees, boards of regents, and the like. In more general terms, John D. Millet describes governance as both a structure and a process whereby basic decisions about purpose, procedures, and performance are made.[9]

In view of this lack of consensus, it seems best to take the Humpty Dumpty approach and devise our own meaning for "governance." In this work, therefore, it will be defined as the means — both structural and procedural — by which *all* the interested individuals, groups, agencies, and governmental units participate in making policy for a community college.

### Background

In the early days, most of the junior colleges were operationally as well as physically part of the local high school. Thus, they automatically came under the same governmental structure as their parent institution. Yet they were from the beginning considered to be colleges, giving rise to the expectation that they would be governed as such. The entire history of community college governance can be viewed as an attempt to blend secondary and higher education practices to suit the peculiar needs of the public two-year college. Surprisingly, the community colleges have come up with little that is truly original in their quest for an appropriate pattern of governance. There have been changes over the years, to be sure, but they have consisted mainly of grafting four-year college practices onto the basic high-school stock.

And that is pretty much where community college governance stands today: somewhere between the structure typical of secondary schools and that common in higher education. Each college is located at a different point along this continuum, depending on a variety of local factors. To start our study of community college governance, then, let's examine the two types of institution which have served it as models.

### Public Schools

When public schools were first established in the Massachusetts Bay Colony, they were considered to be extensions of the home. Everyone, of course, expected to have a say in running them, and thus decisions were made by the entire community at the annual

Town Meeting. When this grew unwieldy, responsibility for the schools — as well as other governmental activities — was delegated to a group of citizens, the Selectmen. Soon the task of running the schools along with all their other duties became too much even for them. Their solution to this problem was a thoroughly modern one: they appointed a committee from among their members to take over the job. From there it was just a step to appointing or electing a separate group of citizens whose sole responsibility was to supervise the schools. In Massachusetts this group is still known as the School Committee; elsewhere it has come to be known as the Board of Education or Board of Trustees.

These early school boards where chosen to *run* the schools, and they carried out their mission faithfully. They chose the teachers, told them what to teach and how to think and act when not teaching, repaired the roof of the school, cut the wood for its stove, and examined the students to see if their investment had been worthwhile. As school districts became larger, however, and the demands placed upon them greater, even the most dedicated group of laymen found they could not tend to all the details of school management. They began to hire professional managers or administrators, to whom they delegated some of their powers and duties. Gradually, they delegated away more and more authority, to the point that, by the mid-twentieth century, little was left for the school boards. They found themselves in the anomalous position of having almost complete power in theory and almost none in actual practice. This was particularly true in the larger districts where it was most difficult for trustees to keep abreast of all that was going on. The top administrators in these schools even had to delegate some of their responsibilities to assistants — principals, business managers, department heads, curriculum coordinators, to name only a few. But the buck seems to have stopped there. Neither faculty nor students were given much chance to participate in running the public schools.

In recent years the pendulum has begun to swing in the opposite direction: the public is demanding that trustees take their schools back from the professionals; teachers are insisting on their right to share in educational policy-making; and students are saying that they too have something valid to contribute to this process. These same forces are operative in the community colleges, bringing about comparable changes in their decision-making structure. But their system of governance — like that of the high schools — remains rooted in the hierarchical, administrator-dominated model typical of the mid-1900's.

### Colleges and Universities

In the United States all institutions of higher education — private as well as public — are considered to be a public trust. Some are directly controlled by a state, a municipality, or a district, while others are controlled by private agencies and operate under charters issued by the government. These charters confer certain powers, privileges, and immunities upon their holders and also spell out their duties and obligations. Authority to direct the affairs of the college or university is given into the hands of some sort of governing board. This board is usually composed of laymen whose duty it is to represent the interests of the sustaining community.

Although the early colleges were tightly controlled by their boards of trustees — much as were the elementary and secondary schools — they too gradually delegated their powers to professional administrators. The temptation for them to follow this path was even greater than for public school trustees: they usually were not local residents, making personal supervision almost impossible; and their amateur status made it difficult for them to operate with confidence in the more esoteric world of higher education. Thus, college and university boards, while retaining extensive powers on paper, in actuality came to exercise very few of them.

Some very strong presidents took full advantage of this situation and exercised almost dictatorial control over their institutions. But, in most cases, they did not retain as much power as did high school administrators. Not only did they delegate certain powers to their aides, but they passed on considerable authority to the faculty as a whole or to the various departments. The amount of delegated power varied depending on size, type of control, and local circumstances, but, on the average, college faculties came to enjoy substantially greater decision-making power than their high school counterparts.

This was due partly to the abdication of power on the part of their governing boards and partly to the existence of a long-standing tradition that college faculties should share in setting educational policies. Burton Clark identifies three concepts of authority which vie for supremacy in American colleges and universities: 1) authority based on the "public trust" concept and exercised by the lay governing board;  2) the bureaucratic or hierarchical authority vested in the administration by delegation from the governing board; and 3) the authority of the faculty based on the theory that they should determine educational policy as well as practice.[10] The interaction among these contending principles has led to the concept of "shared authority" by which most colleges and universities in the United States today are actually governed. This sharing of power, however, did not until very recently extend to the students; despite their added maturity, they were given no more role in the decision-making process than were high school students.

### Fact and Fiction

It's interesting to note that some of the widely-held beliefs about how universities used to be governed — and by implication how they should now be governed — are of doubtful historical authenticity. Once upon a time, so the story goes, university faculties were self-governing communities of scholars, dispensing knowledge to the eager students who came to sit at their feet. Only recently have lay governing boards and professional administrators insinuated themselves into this Garden of Eden, corrupting the natural relationship between teacher and student. The board of trustees is the arch-villain, a diabolical creation of American captains of industry bent upon running the university like a corporation.

Dr. W. H. Cowley's research indicates that this Golden Age was more myth than reality. He invites us to "Consider three long-standing fictions. First, that the academic governing board composed of laymen rather than of professors is an American invention; second, that the academic presidency has no European background or current counterparts; and, third, that wily business tycoons, using the commercial corporation as their model, have foisted lay boards and presidents upon defrauded professors . . .

These and similar statements emanate from a fourth delusive belief; namely that the medieval university, the foundational structure of American colleges and universities, constituted 'a free republic of scholars'."[11] He goes on to show that lay governing boards originated before Columbus set sail for America, that presidents or their equivalents were invented and still exist in Europe, and that faculties were always subject to some kind of outside control, be it by student-elected administrators, civil officials, or the church.[12]

The concept of lay control of higher education — often thought to be of recent origin — turns out to have a long and honorable history. The medieval Italian universities were at first controlled by their students: they paid the professors, chose the administrators, and promulgated the statutes under which the institution operated. But the faculty apparently did not enjoy dancing to the tune of their students; soon they appealed to the civil authorities to contract for their services instead. This the government officials were willing to do, but at the usual price: if they were going to pay, they were going to appoint someone to oversee the use of their money. The Council of Florence established the first such board in 1348; others got underway elsewhere in Italy during the following century.[13] While some of the European universities remained under ecclesiastical control, others adopted this concept of lay supervision developed in Italy. It was eagerly appropriated by Calvin for his Academy in Geneva, since it fit in perfectly with his tenet that laymen should participate in the management of all social institutions. From Geneva it was exported to Holland and thence to Scotland and Ireland; from these countries the early colonists brought it to American shores. Thus, the American way of governing higher education can trace its roots back to the very earliest of European universities.

### Conclusion

Community college governance today is an amalgam of procedures borrowed from the high schools and four-year colleges. The former served as model and mentor during the early years; the latter has more recently assumed this role. Their influence is still strong, but there are signs that it is waning. Community colleges are demanding to be treated differently from both secondary and higher education, insisting that their special characteristics be taken into account in legislation and regulations affecting them. Thus, it may be that even in the area of governance, where their dependency has been so great and has lasted so long, the community colleges are now ready to break away from both high school and university models and go on to develop a style of governance all their own.

*REFERENCES*

[1]J. S. Brubacher and W. Rudy, *Higher Education in Transition,* New York: Harper & Row, 1968, p. 161.

[2]*The Statistical History of the United States from Colonial Times to the Present,* Stamford, Conn.: Fairfield Publishers, Inc., 1965, p. 207.

[3]Quoted in *The Encyclopedia Britannica,* Chicago, Ill.: Encyclopedia Brittanica, Inc., 1965, Vol. 22, p. 875.

[4]*The Statistical History of the United States from Colonial Times to the Present, op. cit.,* pp. 210-211.

[5]C. Blocker, R. Plummer, and R. Richardson, *The Two-Year College: a Social Synthesis,* Englewood Cliffs, N.J.: Prentice-Hall, 1965, p. 24.

[6]C. R. Monroe, *Profile of the Community College: A Handbook,* San Francisco: Jossey-Bass, 1972, p. 9.

[7]*The American Heritage Dictionary of the English Language,* Boston, Mass.; The American Heritage Publishing Co., Inc., and Houghton Mifflin Co., 1970, p. 570.

[8]Quoted in J. Bartlett, *Familiar Quotations,* Boston, Mass.: Little, Brown and Company, 1955, p. 659.

[9]John D. Millet in *Governance and Leadership in Higher Education,* Washington, D.C.: Management Division, Academy for Educational Development, 1974, Vol. 3, No. 9.

[10]Quoted in H. L. Mason, *College and University Government,* New Orleans, La.: Tulane University, 1972, pp. 4-5.

[11]W. H. Cowley, "Professors, Presidents, and Trustees," in *Kennecott Lecture Series,* Tucson, Ariz.: University of Arizona Press, 1962, p. 44.

[12]*Ibid.,* pp. 48-49.

[13]*Ibid.,* pp. 48-49.

# CHAPTER 2
# Federal and State Superstructure

The first question that occurs to a neophyte in community college governance must surely be "Who's in charge here?" An excellent question — and almost impossible to answer. A clue to its complexity is found in a report prepared for California's Coordinating Council for Higher Education: it identifies 54 different local, county, regional, and state organizations or officials to whom the legislature has delegated some degree of responsibility for the community colleges of the state.[1] And this survey doesn't even touch on the rapidly growing federal role in public education. It comes as no surprise, then, that a recent study on the trusteeship of higher education concluded that community college trustees in some ways have the hardest job of all. Not only must they master the very complicated legal structure under which public two-year colleges operate, but they must practically acquire a second language to understand the jargon in which these laws and regulations are written.[2]

## Federal Role

Although we tend to think of community colleges as creatures of local government (a city, a county, a special district), actually every level has a voice in their operation. First comes the federal government, which keeps an eye on the whole show from afar. Although the United States constitution leaves the responsibility for education to the states, Congress and the Supreme Court have become increasingly involved. Their laws and decisions, of course, provide the framework within which all social institutions must operate. Many of them have a very direct and specific effect on the community colleges: integration, dress, due process, free speech, and student records, to name but a few.

For a variety of social reasons, education has recently moved front and center on the stage of American life; in the process, it has increasingly attracted the interest of federal lawmakers. The Office of Education noted on the occasion of its 100th birthday in 1967 that Congress had passed more major pieces of legislation for education in the previous three years than in the preceding 97 combined. Add to this the fact that as the cost of education outstrips the availability of local and state funds, the tendency is to turn to Congress for help. But federal aid, like all other kinds, comes with strings attached. Funds are provided only for those purposes and projects legislators consider worthwhile, and the manner of their use is strictly regulated. Recently there has even been federal intervention in the accreditation process, long a voluntary, professional, regional activity. The rationale: if Congress is to make funds available to the colleges, it is going to monitor their use. All of this is mixed up with the ongoing debate as to how federal aid should be packaged: Should it continue to be given on a categorical basis, i.e., for specific purposes and directly to specific colleges? Or should a lump sum be given to state or local governments to allocate as they see fit? Or should aid be given directly to potential students, who will then decide which institution best meets their needs? There are arguments favoring all sides: Congress is loath to give up the power to decide how *its* money is used, while advocates of decentralization believe units of government closer to the scene or individual students themselves are in a better position to use funds wisely.

### State Role

The really decisive voice in the affairs of a community college is that of the state legislature. Within the limitations imposed by the state and federal constitutions, it literally has the power of life and death over public higher education. The legislature alone decides 1) if there will be community colleges and 2) how they will be governed.

Once a state has decided in favor of community colleges, how

can it exercise control over them? Let us count the ways: it determines their system of governance, establishes the method and level
of funding, regulates their operation via statute and administrative
directive, and charts their future by means of a master plan.

### State Governing Boards

Many states choose to have a centralized community college
system in which all institutions are operated by a state board or as
branches of a state university. At the opposite end of the spectrum
are those states which use the traditional public school pattern:
they delegate the power to maintain community colleges to a unit
of local government. A state-level coordinating board sets the
policy limits within which these local sponsors operate. Even here,
however, the state does not relinquish any of its rights — it can reassume the delegated powers at any time. Still other states occupy
a halfway house: they have state boards which both coordinate
and perform some operating functions, while other powers are assigned to local advisory boards set up for each college.

All three types of state boards — operating, coordinating, and
half-and-half — can be either single-purpose (responsible for community colleges alone) or multi-purpose (responsible for another
level of education as well). Their members may be appointed or
elected, but appointment is the usual route to office.

### Legislation

No matter what governance system they adopt, state lawmakers
jealously guard their right to legislate at any time on any aspect of
community college affairs. Although there is no consistent pattern
nationwide, the following topics are those most frequently covered by state law: conditions for establishing colleges, courses to be
offered, the role of state agencies in operating or coordinating the
colleges, certification of teachers, fiscal procedures and policies,
accreditation standards, budgetary procedures, admissions policies,
tuition charges, physical facilities, and educational standards.[3]

Legislatures also intervene to correct specific abuses or to force
action on recalcitrant (in their eyes) colleges. An example of the
former is the Michigan statute (subsequently voided by the courts)
setting faculty teaching loads; the latter is illustrated by
California's action several years ago requiring all colleges to estab-

lish academic senates and to accord them certain privileges.

Due to its power of the purse (most states provide some community college support, some provide almost all), the legislature can impose whatever requirements it likes via the annual budget, thus exercising continuing control over the most minute details of college operation, if it so desires.

## Other Controls

A whole host of other Big Brothers spend at least part of their time keeping tabs on the community colleges. Many states have a superboard or council charged with coordinating all segments of higher education. Special advisory committees have the task of overseeing vocational education throughout the public school system. The executive branch keeps track of how state monies are spent. State court decisions, attorney generals' opinions, the various departments and regulatory agencies of the state, certain municipal and county governmental units — all these and more at some point have a voice in the affairs of the colleges. And at regular intervals, the regional accrediting agencies look deep into the heart of each institution to determine if it is performing as advertised.

## Expanding State Role

As noted earlier, federal influence on the community colleges is growing rapidly. There is a parallel trend at the state level towards more complete control and coordination of all higher education, including, of course, the community colleges.[4] The primary reason for this shift is economic. Traditionally, community colleges were financed from local sources. A 1929 survey of 30 colleges in several different states found that only three percent of their support came from the state, while 46 percent came from local tax levies. In that same year the Texas legislature passed a law expressly forbidding the use of state school funds for the establishment, support, or maintenance of a junior college. Forty years later — the legislature presumably having undergone a change of heart or of membership — 51 percent of its community college costs were being paid by the state of Texas.[5]

The shift from local to state support was brought about by a combination of factors: skyrocketing enrollments, inflationary pressures, competition with secondary education for local funds, and the assumption of responsibility for educating previously unreached segments of the population.[6] As a result, by the mid-sixties local and state support were approximately equal nationwide, with some 15 states having moved completely away from local support. The tip-over point as far as governance is concerned seems to be at about 60 percent: almost all states providing that much or more state aid assign control of their community colleges to a state agency. An exception may be Florida: in 1968 the legislature moved to complete state funding without changing the locus of control, which was, to a high degree, local.[7]

There are other reasons for the states' growing role in community college governance. As their numbers made them more visible politically, the colleges more frequently attracted the attention of state authorities. Those states that came late to the scene often turned to a centralized system as the fastest way to catch up. Those with a tradition of locally controlled institutions attempted to tighten up their operations in the interests of increased efficiency. In the eyes of state financial experts, the colleges and their local governing boards often are guilty of the deadly sins of "overlapping, duplication, and the unnecessary dispersion of financial resources."[8] And, in the words of one high official, "when individuals and institutions fail to exhibit social responsibility, external agencies impose constraints."[9] He further warns that "in state capitols throughout the land, highly trained staffs . . . are hired and rewarded for carrying out from the state's point of view one important responsibility . . . concern with efficiency."[10]

A case in point are the California community colleges. For fifty years they competed unsuccessfully with the elementary and secondary schools for the attention of the agency charged with their supervision, the State Board of Education. Due to this relative lack of state interest, each college was free to develop pretty much along lines dictated by the local community. The results were, in the words of the Chinese proverb, to "Let a hundred flowers bloom together; let the hundred schools of thought contend." By the 1960's the California community colleges were envied and emulated throughout the world, heralded as the "only truly American institution of education". Although they had reached this pinnacle with a minimum of state involvement, the legislature at that time decided to improve on nature by changing their mode of governance. For the benign neglect of the State Board of Education it substituted the active attention of a separate Board of Governors and a greatly expanded staff. Although the basic commitment to local control was left intact, the potentiality for increased state coordination and control is evident.

John J. Corson sums up the situation with regard to both state and federal control as follows: "The great issue in the governance of higher education in the 1970s is not the struggle over who has power on the campus: students, faculty, administrators or trustees. The great issue is how the individual college or university can retain the power needed for effective governance, while government groups (state coordinating councils, superboards, legislatures, budget officers, governors' offices and Federal agencies — particularly HEW) expand their controls in the name of coordination, economy, and individual rights."[11]

### Local Influences on the State

So far the relationship between the state and the individual college has appeared to be a one-way street, with the former actively imposing its will and the latter passively accepting it. This would make of the state some sort of computerized monster, responsive only to its own internal program. State government is, of course, simply a collection of people, and — most importantly — people who have to stand for election at regular intervals or who are appointed by those who do. As such, they must be responsive to their constituents, among whom are many with a special interest in community colleges. In the next chapter we will explore the ways in which constituents influence their elected representatives and their appointees; suffice it to say that college trustees and staff *can* affect state-level actions.

Effective action, however, requires organization. Obviously, the larger the unit of government, the less likely it is to respond to the blandishments of a single constituent. For an idea to have a major impact, its sponsors must show that large numbers of people are behind it. Thus, community colleges have had to band together to make their influence felt in legislative halls and executive offices.

Statewide organizations come in all shapes and sizes, ranging from the brand-new Maryland community college trustees' association with its 13 member-Boards to the giant California Community and Junior College Association. The latter has a 36-member Board of Directors composed of equal numbers of faculty, administrators, students, and trustees, a full-time staff of ten, and an annual budget of a quarter of a million dollars. Between these two extremes comes a veritable alphabet soup of state organizations. Faculty have academic senates, faculty associations, branches of all the well-known national groups — AAUP, AFT, NEA — and a myriad of discipline-oriented organizations. Administrators have specialized groups representing every known sub-species — deans, business managers, publicity directors, financial aid officers, you name it. Students usually work together through a statewide student government association. And trustees have the choice of working with Board members at other levels of the educational system, joining with community college administrators and teachers, or establishing groups of their own.

Although these associations are not set up solely — or even primarily — to influence state-level actions, they play an important role in this arena. Often they have spokesmen — paid or volunteer — in the state capital whose job it is to watch, inform, and cajole members of the legislature, the state governing board, and the regulatory agencies. In times of crisis they can marshall an impressive show of grass-roots strength from their membership around the state. Together members of these groups have a political clout which they would never be able to muster individually.

### Local Influence on the Federal Government

A parallel structure exists at the national level. Most of the organizations already described either are branches of nationwide associations or have their national counterparts. There must be some law of nature to the effect that the farther one is from the scene of action, the harder it is to affect that action. Since most community colleges are located quite a way from Washington, D.C., the difficulties involved in this long-distance political action seem almost insurmountable. To strengthen the community college "presence" there, the American Association of Community and Junior Colleges (AACJC) has recently undergone a major reorganization, and trustees have banded together to form the rapidly growing Association of Community College Trustees (ACCT).

As the federal role in higher education expands still further, there will be a continuing search for more effective ways of influencing it.

## Conclusion

The primary responsibility for public education, including the community colleges, rests with the states. Traditionally, they have parceled out the powers and duties attendant upon this responsibility to a wide variety of governmental agencies and units. The power to establish and operate community colleges was usually delegated to local government – a municipality, a county, or a special district. Although a certain amount of control and co-ordination took place at the state level, the major locus of power was local. In recent years, however, the trend has been for the states and the federal government to exercise greater control over the community colleges. Leaders in the field deplore this, fearing that it will lead to the loss of those qualities they prize most highly: the opportunity to experiment, to change, to be different from each other and from other educational institutions. Recognizing that a very real need exists to assure the efficient use of available monies, the task ahead is to find a way to do this without destroying the peculiar genius of the community colleges.

---

*REFERENCES*

[1]"Problems and Perceptions on Control and Coordination," Report to the Board of Directors of the California Junior College Association, September 12, 1973, p. 1.

[2] M. A. Rauh, *The Trusteeship of Colleges and Universities,* New York: McGraw-Hill, 1969, pp. 132-133.

[3]Blocker et al, *op. cit.,* p. 85.

[4]*Ibid.,* p. 100.

[5]J. L. Wattenbarger, W.N. Holcombe, S. L. Myrick, and C. R. Paulson, "State-Local Financing for the Seventies," in J. Lombardi (Ed.), *Meeting the Financial Crisis,* San Francisco: Jossey-Bass, 1973, pp. 1-3.

[6]*Ibid.,* pp. 5-8.

[7]*Ibid.*, pp. 3-4.

[8]Blocker et al, *op. cit.*, p. 100.

[9]Alex C. Sherriffs, "Whose Decision?," speech delivered at the Carnegie Commission/AGB Regional Seminar, St. Francis Hotel, San Francisco, California, June 15, 1972, p. 10.

[10]*Ibid.*, p. 9.

[11]John J. Corson, "Institutional Governance within a System," *Educational Record,* Spring 1973, Vol. 54:2, pp. 107-114, p. 107.

# CHAPTER 3
# Local Structure

When a state decides to delegate the power to operate community colleges to a unit of local government, it can do so in one of several ways. The legislature can create special districts with authority only to operate two-year colleges; it can permit pre-existing school districts to establish colleges; or it can extend this privilege to cities or counties. The residents of any one of these local political units constitute the college's "community." When a state operates its colleges directly, the whole state is looked upon as a single community.

## Powers of the People

Whichever pattern of local control is adopted, the powers delegated by the state are divided between the electorate and a governing board. A majority of the voters must usually give their permission to form a college district and to make subsequent boundary changes. They also have the right to elect and recall board members, or, at least, to have them appointed by officials they do elect. The public exercises continuing control over the colleges via the power of the purse. Although each state uses a different mixture of taxes (state, local, property, income, permissive, voted) to support its colleges, voters often have the opportunity to say yea or nay to a special tax levy or budget proposal. They are even more likely to have this prerogative with regard to major construction projects, which are frequently financed by bond issues requiring a vote of the people.

## Powers of the Governing Board

Short of a court order requiring the commission or cessation of a certain act, the public has no other direct way to impose its will upon the college. All else it wishes to accomplish must be done through its major instrument of control, the board of trustees.

Even the founding fathers, you will recall, soon found it was impractical for the entire town to participate directly in running the schools. As a result, it became customary to entrust their supervision to a specially chosen group of citizens. These "trustees" are either elected by the people or chosen by other officials (mayors, governors, state legislatures, city councilmen) who have themselves been elected. The terms of office of community college trustees are relatively short — three to six years on the average — permitting the electorate to evaluate their performance at regular intervals. If they get out of line in the interim, in most states they can be recalled in midterm: although drastic, this procedure is frequently used by a community unhappy with the actions of its public officials.

The local governing board has complete authority for organizing and operating community colleges — within limits. Its duties and responsibilities are spelled out in some detail in legislation, in administrative directives, and in court decisions.[1] Basically, its powers include the right to own property, to levy taxes, to sue and be sued in the courts, and to make all necessary rules for the governance of the colleges under its jurisdiction.[2] The amount of latitude permitted local boards varies widely from state to state. Some, for example, permit them to take any college-related action that is not expressly *forbidden* by state law or regulation, while others permit them to take only those actions that are expressly *authorized* by the state.

The most widely agreed upon characteristic of school board power today is that it is in the process of change. Initially, local boards possessed extensive legislative and executive authority. They made the policy and they implemented it, hiring and promoting teachers, buying textbooks, and the like. During the second half of the nineteenth century they were pretty well stripped of their executive powers, yielding them to professional administrators. More recently, federal and state governments have encroached even on their legislative function by passing ever-more restrictive laws and establishing regulatory agencies. The power of individual boards has been further eroded by the growth of a body of universally accepted policy on education issues at the state and national level. Some feel that they have in reality been reduced to simply fulfilling a judicial function, to deciding what rule or law is applicable in a given local situation. Their range of discretion is further circumscribed by local social and economic conditions, which determine the financial parameters within which their decision-making takes place.[3]

While the powers of boards of trustees have been contracting, the role of the institutions for which they are responsible has been expanding. Formerly, schools were held responsible for "instructing a given clientele of a given age range in the use of a few basic intellectual tools."[4] This description is hardly recognizable to the community college trustee of today. Due to a variety of social changes, the boundaries of college responsibility have become progressively blurred. America looks to its schools for the solution of major social problems: poverty, racial discrimination, and automation, to name but a few. This trend was first evident at the elementary and secondary level but spread rapidly to the community colleges as well. Board agendas today are replete with topics unheard of two decades ago; what board does not deal with health care, psychiatric services, legal aid, child care centers, free lunches, financial aid, and special programs for women, minority racial and ethnic groups, and the physically handicapped? Community colleges try to serve the needs of citizens of all ages, from 18 to 80. Not only do they no longer cater to an elite in terms of age, socioeconomic class, or intellectual ability, but they are expected to prepare the "whole man" for living as well as working in today's world. This is a heavy burden to lay upon even the most powerful of social institutions − let alone the community colleges, with their relatively limited ability to respond.

### Perception of Board Powers

The public's perception of board powers is in line with its expectations for the college: it thinks they can do much more than they really can. This chasm between appearance and reality can spell real trouble for trustees. Critics rant and rave at the board for its failure to impose higher tuition, to reduce the number of hours devoted to physical education, or to provide housing for the disadvantaged — only to find that it has no authority to do any of these things. This does not mitigate their annoyance with the local board, since they have no one else nearby on whom to vent their anger. Equally disappointed with the board's performance are the starry-eyed reformers who approach it with requests for help in stopping wars, halting atmospheric pollution, and ending man's inhumanity to man. Their excessive estimate of trustees' power is matched only by that of the ultraconservatives, who expect the board to magically turn back the clock so that today's students think, look, and act like their grandparents.

Sometimes, however, this distorted notion of the local board's power redounds to its credit: a reduction in the local tax rate made possible by increased state aid, an affirmative action policy required by the federal government, or a new vocational program mandated by the state are all attributed to the wisdom of the local trustees. Even trustees themselves have an inflated view of their own authority: a recent survey showed that board members in one state assumed they had many powers that were in fact legally reserved for the state coordinating board.[5]

Not only do local boards lack the power to do many things the citizenry expects of them, but they may even be required to do some things their constituents do not like. Their role as an instrument of state control of education is rarely understood: thus conflict may erupt when the board tries to enforce an unpopular statute or judicial decision.[6] A case in point is the elementary board of trustees which attempted to comply with the Supreme Court ruling banning prayer in the schools. Only three of the five members could bring themselves to vote in favor of directing teachers not to conduct prayers; those three were subsequently recalled by an irate community for accepting their responsibility to carry out the law of the land.[7] Community college trustees find themselves in similar dilemmas in sensitive areas such as dress codes, speakers on campus, and censorship of student publications.

The frustrations experienced by trustees attempting to do an almost unlimited job of education with severely limited powers are great. It is for this reason that many of them are induced to spend large amounts of time working individually and through organizations to modify the "superstructure" within which they operate. Their goal is twofold: to bring to the attention of state and national authorities the problems encountered on the local level and to seek legislation and regulations that will permit the community colleges to respond more adequately to the needs of their constituents. At the same time it should be recognized that the view from the state capitals and from Washington is somewhat different: lawmakers there feel that their better overall perspective qualifies them at least as well as local trustees to act in the best interests of the community colleges.

## Conclusion

The locus of control for each community college is determined by the organizational plan adopted by the state in which it is located. The state may operate its two-year colleges directly or assign this power to a unit of local government. Even if the latter alternative is chosen, the local sponsor does not have complete control; it operates within the limits set by state laws and regulations, and certain powers are reserved for the state's coordinating board. Additionally, when the responsible political unit – state or local – operates more than one institution, each college may have its own advisory committee with substantial recommending powers. Thus, decision-making power on any given aspect of community college affairs may reside at the institutional, the local, or the state level - or be shared by all three.

*REFERENCES*

[1] Blocker, *op. cit.*, p. 88.

[2] Monroe, *op. cit.*, pp. 306-307.

[3] H.T. James, "School Board Conflict is Inevitable," *American School Board Journal*, March 1967, pp. 6-7.

[4] D.W. Minar, "Community Politics and School Boards," *American School Board Journal*, March 1967, p. 31.

[5] "Problems and Perceptions on Control and Coordination," *op. cit.*, p. 9.

[6] James, *op. cit.*, p. 6.

[7] *Ibid.*, p. 6.

# CHAPTER 4
# The Voice
# of the Community

The key to the uniqueness of the public two-year college is found in the name by which it has come to be known: the community college. The dictionary offers a wide choice of meanings for the word "community," including a "group of people living in the same locality and under the same government" and "a body of people having common interests."[1] Using the second definition, even private institutions might qualify as "community" colleges, since they tend to serve certain affinity groups within our society. Some, for example, cater to members of a particular religious denomination, others to an intellectual elite, and still others to a certain social or economic class. Theirs is, however, a rather casual, take-it-or-leave-it arrangement, with the colleges free to change their emphasis and the students to take their business wherever they like. Neither has any real control over the other: the college cannot force students to choose it over another school; students cannot demand that they be accepted or that the courses they want be offered.

The true community college, on the other hand, must serve *all* the people "living in the same locality and under the same government." Notice that nothing is said about "common interests"; indeed, the reverse is more often the case, with extreme heterogeneity the hallmark of the populace served by many a community college. Its relationship to its constituents is very different from that of a private college, a marriage rather than a liaison, so to speak. College and community have certain legal obligations to each other: the former must provide educational services for residents of a designated area, while the latter must provide the wherewithal for the college to operate. Everyone living in the area — whether or not he or she ever attends the college — is required to contribute to its support via state or local taxes. Thus, everyone has an interest in the economy — if not the quality — of its operation. The college's governing board (if locally controlled) or advisory committee (if state-run) is composed of local residents, assuring a high degree of community involvement in the governance process. And, most importantly, its students seldom can go elsewhere if they don't like what the local college offers. A combination of legal residency requirements and financial considerations effectively bars most citizens from shopping around for a community college to their liking. Thus, it is essential that local residents be able to create the kind of college that best serves their particular needs.

### Citizen Participation in Trustee Elections

The very best way for citizens to have an impact on their community college is to be elected to its board of trustees. The second best way is to elect someone they trust to represent them on this board.

This being the case, why do so few people vote in trustee elections? This malady — apathy by name — afflicts all levels of democratic government in our country. Although everyone knows the President of the United States has a great deal of power to affect their lives, only 55.7 percent of the voting age population exercised their prerogative in the 1972 presidential election.[2] In interviews after the November 1974 state, local, and congressional elections, less than 45 percent of the people reported that they had voted. The turnout in local trustee elections is often far smaller still. In many places, 20 percent is considered a good turnout, permitting a trustee to win by receiving the votes of just over 10 percent of the people — even less if there are several candidates and no run-off requirement.

This is hardly a new phenomenon: Will Rogers remarked fifty years ago that "It's just got so that 90 percent of the people in this country don't give a damn. Politics ain't worrying this country one-tenth as much as parking space." Modern political analysts confirm the great humorist's insights. One divides the population into Gladiators, Spectators, and Apathetics: "The Gladiators . . . constituting something like a tenth of the population, are the political activists. Under normal conditions, the rest of the electorate permits a small group to govern with relatively little interference, consulting only with the particular interest groups directly affected by their decisions. When crises arise . . . the larger group of Spectators enters the political arena . . . the Apathetics, roughly a third of the electorate, seldom participate in political activities and usually do not even vote."[3] One author states bluntly that "It would clear the air of a good deal of cant if instead of assuming that politics is a normal and natural concern of human beings, one were to make the contrary assumption that, whatever lip service citizens may pay to platitudes, politics is a remote, alien, and unrewarding activity."[4]

Since many, if not all, elected trustees are really chosen by a minority of the voters, can they truly be said to represent the entire community? The answer lies hidden in the minds of the no-shows: why don't they vote? Because they know too little about the issues to do so intelligently? Because they don't care what kind of college they have? Because they like the *status quo* and assume that it will continue without any effort on their part?

The answer seems to be that *many, if not most, people couldn't care less about governing themselves.* They're more than happy to leave it up to someone else unless and until things get out of hand. When that happens, when some invisible boundary is crossed, aroused communities can and do turn out tremendous number of voters. Studies indicate a direct relationship between the level of participation in elections and the level of dissent in a school district: the more people going to the polls, the higher the dissenting vote.[5] In the absence of this indication of concern, however, we can only assume that trustees are doing an adequate job of reflecting the thinking of their community.

### Influencing the Board of Trustees

Fortunately, the concerned public doesn't just choose a board of trustees and then go fishing until the next election rolls around. Many issues come up during trustees' terms which neither they nor the voters could have foreseen during the campaign; as a result, no one knows how they stand on these matters. Also, trustees (male as well as female) in all good faith change their minds after assuming office and take positions opposed to those espoused prior to election. Some trustees even owe their victory to the skillful avoidance of controversial subjects while campaigning. Others win by spending more money than their opponents; still others are elected because they are esteemed for their achievements in fields totally unrelated to community colleges.

For all of these reasons, trustees' actions cannot be accurately predicted on the basis of pre-election information alone. Citizens must take care to communicate with them regularly during their terms of office to make sure their mandates are understood and executed. Eternal vigilance is everywhere the price of responsive and responsible government.

### Citizens' Advisory Committees

Many boards actively solicit the opinions of local citizens by appointing advisory committees. No governing board of manageable size can hope to have every point of view represented by its members alone, nor do they have a monopoly on good ideas for making the college responsive to the community. Advisory committees are a means of extending the board's antennae out into the community, of multiplying the opportunities for interaction between the college and its constituency.

Such committees can be either permanent or temporary: the former are useful for programs requiring continuing surveillance and updating (vocational, recreational, multicultural); the latter are best for meeting specific, nonrecurring needs (financial crises, problems with neighbors, changing district boundaries). The strength of the board's desire for community involvement can be determined by the number and calibre of its advisory groups. If they are few in number and packed with known college supporters, with friends of trustees and staff, their advice will be predictable and comfortable. If they are numerous and include representatives picked by the many different interest groups and organizations in the community, their advice may be unpredictable and even unpleasant, but it will reflect the thinking of the general public. An extension of the advisory committee approach is to invite citizens to become involved along with college staff and trustees on a continuing basis; this system is known as "participatory planning" or "participatory management."6

### Access to Information

If interested members of the community want to influence their college, they must first know what's going on. This is a difficult assignment even for trustees (as a later chapter will show), let alone for the general public. Their greatest ally is the open board meeting, where all official business must be transacted. A recent survey indicated that some 89 percent of public institutions of higher education do in fact have such open meetings.[7] Admittedly, a dedicated board and staff can find ways of getting around this requirement: touchy issues can be discussed in executive session or at informal get-togethers. This, however, requires the collusion of all present, since disclosure by even one member would bring the wrath of the public — and, in some states, of the law — down upon the heads of the participants.

The public's "right to know" is also protected by legal requirements for advertising meetings, bids, and budgets, and the right to inspect all public records. The best safeguard of all is a vigorous and responsible press. Most people count on the local newspaper, through investigative reporting as well as board meeting coverage, to alert them to happenings of particular interest. By far the most effective publicizers of the college are its many students, who spread their perceptions and opinions throughout the community.

### Mechanics of Community Involvement

Assuming, then, that interested citizens can find out what's going on at the college, how do they make their reactions and suggestions known to members of the governing board? One obvious way is by direct, personal contact. Such contacts range from phone messages from anonymous callers to chance meetings at the supermarket (women) or service club (men) to long discussions with close friends. The content of these communications runs the gamut from statements of support and encouragement to threats to life and limb. If the composition of the board closely parallels that of the community it serves, random contacts can be a good indication of public sentiment. If not, other means must be utilized to assure a balanced flow of information to the policy-makers.

On matters of major importance or of long-standing interest, the public makes its wishes known through collective action. Some organizations have a permanent interest in school affairs and monitor them on a regular basis — the League of Women Voters and taxpayers' associations, for example. Others, often bearing names like "Citizens for the College Bond Issue" or "Coalition to Protest Parking Fees," are formed to lobby for or against a specific proposal. Some have memberships that are themselves a microcosm of the community; their recommendations are a good indication of public sentiment. Others represent a specific segment of the populace only; their names usually provide a clue to their makeup, but some try to mask their true identity by adopting a misleading title.

One study analyzed the frequency with which various organizations and individuals attempted to bring pressure to bear on a group of some 500 school board members. Although this survey did not include community college trustees, the mechanics of citizen participation are similar at all levels of the public educational system. Thus, with a few modifications, the results can be considered applicable to community colleges as well.

The most active "outside" (that is, exclusive of teachers and other trustees) group by far — making over twice as many contacts as any other single category — consisted of parents and parents' associations. At the community college level, this category would consist of students as well as their parents. Other groups in order of frequency were:

1.   City or town officials
2.   Personal friends
3.   Taxpayers' associations
4.   Politicians
5.   Old-line families
6.   Economically influential citizens
7.   The press
8.   Business or commercial organizations

plus every other imaginable group, again in order: churches, service clubs, veterans' associations, fraternal organizations, labor unions, chambers of commerce, and farm and welfare organizations.[8]

Another recent survey found that interest *groups* (individuals were not considered here) came to the attention of school boards in the following order:

1. PTA - still far out in front of all the rest
2. Left-wing and civil-rights groups
3. Service clubs
4. Business and professional organizations
5. Taxpayers
6. Right-wing groups
7. League of Women Voters
8. Religious organizations

plus citizens' advisory committees, and political, neighborhood, and labor organizations.[9] This study says nothing about content of these contacts or their effectiveness. Another survey, however, concluded that the community connections of board members — personal, fraternal, social, professional, and business — had a definite bearing on the decisions they made. The evidence also showed that while some trustees were considerably swayed by this influence, particularly on current as opposed to long-range issues, others tended to ignore it.[10]

Trustees are most likely to go along with a request from a constituent if it is in line with their own personal convictions. Cynics to the contrary notwithstanding, holders of public office do have principles. It would be very difficult, for example, to talk an ardent ACLU member into taking an action restricting the freedom of the college newspaper; nor could a known super-patriot be easily persuaded to vote for the elimination of the daily pledge-to-the-flag ceremony.

Trustees are people and therefore subject to the same human frailties as the rest of the species. They are more likely to be responsive to their friends than to their enemies, to someone to whom they owe a favor than to someone they've never heard of before. They feel particularly indebted to those who help them get elected, to those who were willing to go out on a limb for them *before* they achieved the power and prestige of office. If they have a large constituency, aspiring trustees must usually go outside of their immediate circle of family and friends for campaign help. They are grateful to those who come forward to aid in this endeavor — and, if elected, anxious to do something in return. It should be noted that this campaign "help" is by no means limited to financial contributions; those workers who give generously of their time are valued at least as highly as those who write the checks.

Another route to the board's heart is via the press: both news coverage and editorial opinions can influence trustees' actions. The "Letters to the Editor" column can be used to enlist the public in a crusade to support or oppose board positions. Groups also invoke the sacred American right to petition their public officials; it is an unwise board indeed that does not give careful attention to such presentations. The technique of packing board meetings with supporters of a particular cause is increasingly in vogue. The real purpose of this approach is intimidation: clearly two people can present a group's position as well as 200. But the impact, at least in the short run, of a crowd of angry constituents is admittedly greater than that of a handful of polite representatives.

### Politics!

It should be evident by now that we are leaving the Real World behind and entering into the Never-Never Land of politics. Fortunately the day is past when everyone piously declared that "politics and education don't mix" and " we must keep politics out of our schools." Today one is more likely to hear that "education is one of the most thoroughly political enterprises in American life"[11] or "School politics cannot be isolated from the politics of other public and private agencies operating within the local school district."[12]

"Politics," of course, can mean many different things, depending on the context in which it is used. Here it refers to "the organization or action of individuals, parties, or interests that seek to control the appointment or action of those who manage the affairs of a state."[13] The "state" can be any unit of government — for our purposes, it is whatever unit governs the local college. Translated into terms applicable to community college governance, "politics" is the process whereby members of the community seek to select or influence whatever governing board has the power to manage the college.

Many different ways of exercising this influence have been described: campaign assistance, personal contacts with trustees, presentations at meetings, collective action, press campaigns, and the like. There are those, however — sociologists in the main — who scoff at all this as just so much window dressing. They believe that in most communities, and at the state and national levels as well, the important decisions are all made behind the scenes by a "power elite." This group supposedly manipulates the elected representatives of the people at will through its economic power, which adherents of this thesis consider to be the critical basis of community control.[14]

Political scientists, however, tend to deny the existence of a single, united economic clique and find instead that power is shared by many competing groups. They consider the power structure to be pluralistic, much more complex and diversified than the "power elite" proponents give it credit for. Adherents of this "multi-influence" theory hold that many different groups and individuals are able to make their influence felt in the policy-making process.[15] Dr. Victor Baldridge sums up this controversy — and perhaps lays it to rest — by saying that ". . . it is increasingly plausible that the 'Pluralism vs. power elite' debate is unnecessarily polarized . . . the either-or question is misleading and the more fruitful research asks about relative distribution of power, and about the patterns that emerge. This allows for coexisting elite groups, fragmented spheres of influence, and inter-connected networks of power to be seen as all part of a very complex pattern."[16]

These theories of citizen participation are of particular significance to those in the community colleges because of their pride in maintaining close ties with the constituency they serve. The main thing is to recognize that politics are part and parcel of the democratic decision-making process and thus inextricably intertwined with community college governance.

### Education vs. Partisan Politics

Educational policy-making, however, does exhibit certain distinctive characteristics. Primary among these is its nonpartisanship.

The myth that the schools are apolitical probably originated here, since most Americans tend to identify politics with partisanship. School politics are also set apart because their geographical boundaries differ from those of other local governmental units, their elections are scheduled at different times of year, and their financing comes under separate legal provisions. Educators — and often their lay associates as well — have traditionally done their utmost to erect a stockade around the schools, to insist that educational issues be treated as if they were not related to other matters of public concern. This separation of school and state originated in the reform movements of the late nineteenth and early twentieth centuries. The evils associated with local partisan politics at that time — corruption, bossism, and political machines — led to the feeling that the public school system should be sheltered from the contaminating influence of politics.[17] And last, but by no means least, the fact that it deals with young people gives education an emotional coloration that other governmental activities lack. As Zeigler and Jennings aptly put it, ". . . no single word better describes the American attitude toward education than *reverence*. Education has been the means to realize the American Dream."[18]

For all these reasons the schools have been somewhat removed from the hurly-burly of everyday politics. The role usually played by the political parties is assumed by the various interest groups operating in the community. They form *ad hoc* alliances as the situation demands, then drift apart until the need for concerted action again appears. Their *modus operandi* is to achieve consensus behind the scenes rather than debating problems openly before the public. One author calls this the "politics of the priesthood rather than the hustings." The latter are highly visible and thrive on the conflict and confrontation of campaigns, while the former are hidden and attempt to reach agreement informally prior to open forums or board meetings.[19]

A major point of difference between school and partisan politics is the lack of a permanent opposition. In partisan politics the other party is always there, carping away, day in and day out, in good times as in bad. Those in power expect this criticism and are prepared to react to it. The schools, on the other hand, tend to fear conflict, to try and suppress it at all costs. This lack of on-going, organized criticism of the schools makes it harder for the public's representatives, the board of trustees, to receive the appropriate signals from their constituents.

But times are changing, and school politics are coming more and more to resemble the partisan variety. This is due mainly to changes in American society which are making the "Gentleman's Agreement" type of politics no longer viable. Among these are the growing role of education in determining access to the good life, the increased mobility of the populace, and the demand for participation on the part of formerly quiescent segments of the population. Many observers feel that it would be better if conflicts were brought out into the open, if boards of trustees concentrated on managing rather than avoiding them. This is, in fact, happening in many areas: battles for control of the educational decision-making apparatus are taking place openly for the first time. It may well be that even in the educational field the politics of consensus is gradually giving way to the politics of conflict resolution.

## Conclusion

Community colleges vary widely in philosophy, in size, in form of governance – in almost every conceivable way. But they have one important thing in common: a very close relationship with their constituency. The community creates and sustains the college and determines the nature of the educational services it provides. It exercises control over the college through the political process. Here is the key to the community colleges' special sensitivity to the wishes of their constituents, a characteristic that makes them unique among institutions of higher education. Since politics is the way in which people (the community) choose and control those who manage their institutions (the colleges), it would be a real tragedy if a way were found to keep politics *out* of the community colleges.

---

[1] *The American Heritage Dictionary of the English Language, op. cit.,* p. 270.

[2] U. S. Bureau of the Census, *Statistical Abstract of the U.S.: 1974* (95th Edition), Washington, D.C., 1974, p. 438.

[3]T. R. McConnell, "Faculty Government," in H. L. Hodgkinson and L.R. Meath, Ed., *Power and Authority: Transformation of Campus Governance,* San Francisco, Calif., Jossey-Bass, 1971, pp. 102-3.

[4]R. Dahl, quoted in V. Baldridge, *Power and Conflict in the University,* New York: John Wiley & Sons, 1971, p. 177.

[5]D. W. Minar, *op. cit.,* pp. 33-34.

[6]W. Thompson, "Can Trustees Really Represent Their Communities?" *Community and Junior College Journal* 44:2, Oct. 1973, pp. 13-14.

[7]M. A. Rauh, *op. cit.,* p. 169.

[8]A. Rosenthal (Ed.), *Governing Education,* Garden City, N.Y.: Anchor Books, Doubleday & Co., 1969, pp. 92-93.

[9]L. H. Zeigler and M.K. Jennings, *Governing American Schools,* North Scituate, Mass: Duxbury Press, 1974, p. 99.

[10]K. Goldhammer, *The School Board,* New York: Center for Applied Research in Education, 1964, pp. 84-85.-

[11]A. Rosenthal, *op. cit.,* pp. ix-x.

[12]*Ibid.,* 133-134.

[13]*Webster's New Collegiate Dictionary,* Springfield, Mass: G. & C. Merriam Company, 1961, p. 654.

[14]A. M. Rose, *The Power Structure,* New York: Oxford University Press, 1967, pp. 1-39.

[15]*Ibid.,* pp. 492-493.

[16]V. Baldridge, *Academic Governance,* Berkeley, Calif.: McCutcheon Publishing Corp., 1971, pp. 312-313.

[17]L. H. Zeigler and M.K. Jennings, *op. cit.,* p. 2.

[18]*Ibid,* p. 2.

[19]I. Iannaccone and F. Lutz, "The Changing Politics of Education," *AAUW Journal,* May 1967, p. 161.

# CHAPTER 5
# Hillsdale
# Meets the Needs of
# Its Changing Community

*Note: This chapter, along with chapters VIII and X, is a figment of the author's imagination, created to illustrate the facts and theories set forth in the rest of the book. All incidents and situations described therein, however, are based on real-life happenings.*

In 1955 the junior college movement was just coming into its own in the western states. Most people were enthusiastic about the idea of establishing a public college, convinced that its benefits would far outweigh its costs. In a few communities, however, junior colleges were established primarily in self-defense, to keep a neighboring college from annexing their land and their tax base. This was the case with Hillsdale College. Located in the far-out suburbs of a major metropolitan center, its geographical area was large and its population small. Its residents numbered barely 50,000 and were mainly upper middle-class refugees from the city plus large agriculturists or the speculators who had bought them out. The only place even resembling a "poverty pocket" was San Cristobal, the center of the area's still healthy fruit-growing and processing industry.

During the early years Hillsdale's revenues were consistently high in relation to its student population. The latter remained low because many of the young people went to private colleges, others attended the state university located less than an hour away, and the residents of San Cristobal — mostly of Mexican-American background — often did not even finish high school, let alone contemplate attending college.

From the beginning the idea was to offer a minimal program, to duplicate the lower division courses at the university and no more. There were several reasons for this: most people expected their children to go on for the B.A. degree, it gave the junior college a respectable image in the eyes of the public, and it was cheap. The seven original trustees espoused this philosophy in their campaigns for office and were elected on that basis. They hired a president, Dr. Scott Wilkinson, who shared their views and he, in turn, sought faculty members whose primary interest lay in college-transfer education. Many of those chosen, in fact, saw the junior college as a stepping-stone to their eventual goal of university teaching. The ideal location of Hillsdale College and its proximity to a prestigious university brought many fine applicants for the available positions, and those picked were of the highest caliber.

All went well in this Garden of Eden for the first decade. As the population pushed outward from the city, both the number of citizens  and the tax base from which operating revenues were derived grew. A beautiful campus was built in the foothills along the northern edge of the district. In response to pressures from the state Community College Coordinating Board, a few "high-class" vocational programs — in business, health care, and electronics — were gradually added. Students wishing other vocational curriculums were permitted to attend neighboring colleges. Few did so, however, since this option was not widely advertised and the distances involved were great.

Unremarked by those closest to the college, however, storm clouds were gathering. By 1968 the population of Hillsdale's service area had mushroomed from 50,000 to almost 250,000. San Cristobal alone had gone from a hamlet of 2500 to a near-metropolis of 85,000. The fruit-growing industry had practically been wiped out as subdivisions displaced orchards, but it remained a center for food-processing. The real spur to San Cristobal's growth, however, came in 1964 with the opening of an automobile assembly plant employing thousands. It provided jobs for the Mexican-Americans previously employed in agriculture as well as for blue-collar workers attracted from all over the country by the climate and the employment possibilities. To house them and the overflow from the still-growing metropolis nearby, many of the large ranches were converted into tracts with small homes on minuscule lots. Due to the crazy-quilt pattern of towns in the area and the almost total lack of an overall zoning plan, sections housing the affluent alternated with those providing homes for those of modest means. All this, of course, meant that the socioeconomic profile of the citizenry had changed markedly in the decade since Hillsdale was founded.

There were some warning signals to indicate that Hillsdale College could no longer ignore these changes. Recent elections had brought to the Board of Trustees two members – Roger Merkens and Raul Lopez – who were not totally satisfied with the *status quo*. The latest accreditation report had pointed out serious deficiencies in the vocational program along with the admonition to expand them as quickly as possible. The state Community College Coordinating Board was also making noises to this effect: Hillsdale's required five-year Master Plan had been rejected as inadequate due to its lack of vocational planning. The state's annual survey of the racial and ethnic composition of community college student bodies showed that Hillsdale had enrolled proportionately many fewer Mexican-Americans than were living in its area. Although the state legislature had appropriated special monies for the disadvantaged, Hillsdale's one application for a grant had been turned down because there was no evidence of any local commitment to serve this group. A few trustees had remarked that Hillsdale's lack of interest in vocational courses was costing it plenty in terms of lost federal grants. The last meeting of the state Trustees' Association had described several of the special programs for minority students functioning throughout the state. The newsletter of the state Faculty Association, the *Journal* of the American Association of Junior Colleges, and the metropolitan newspaper's reporting on neighboring colleges brought news of activities in the outside world to the Hillsdale staff and trustees.

These problems all came to a head during the budget discussions. For the first time, the college was faced with an unfavorable financial situation. The state legislature had not seen fit to pump any additional monies into the community colleges that year, despite their growing student bodies and rising costs due to inflation. The administrative staff had finally become convinced that it had to make some gesture in the vocational area. The state Finance Bureau, charged with allocating funds to the community colleges, was threatening to penalize Hillsdale unless it complied with the regulations requiring the adoption of an approved Master Plan. In another two years there would be an accreditation visit, at which time evidence of progress would have to be produced. Several of the trustees had reported that an occasional constituent complained that Hillsdale did not seem to have nearly as much to offer as some of the surrounding colleges.

Meanwhile, others in the Hillsdale community were recognizing its deficiencies in providing educational opportunities for certain segments of the population. Raul Lopez, a successful small businessman from San Cristobal, had been elected to the Board two years before. He did not think of himself particularly as a spokesman for his fellow Mexican-Americans, but he was familiar with their needs. As advocates of minority rights became more vocal, Lopez was pushed by militant members of his group to become more outspoken on their behalf. He soon learned of the special programs offered at other colleges and realized that Hillsdale was really behind the times. When the state report on the student body makeup came out, Lopez publicly demanded that something be done about it. He was joined in this appeal by Roger Merkens, a liberal young lawyer, who suggested establishing what he called a "College Transition Program" for disadvantaged students.

As word reached the students, the Political Action Caucus, an organization dedicated to change on the American political scene, took up the cry. Joining with the Mexican-American Alliance, the Asian Students United, and the small but effective Black Students at Hillsdale, they approached the Student Council for help. This was clearly a popular item and the concept of a College Transition Program was endorsed by acclamation. The vice-president of the Council urged her colleagues to support the expansion of vocational offerings as well. She argued that truly poor students must first learn a skill that will permit them to earn a decent living; only then can they consider taking advantage of the more esoteric college offerings. Despite her eloquent plea, she was turned down. Many Council members just didn't know any students who wanted vocational training that badly, and others thought it was all a plot to supply fodder for the country's military-industrial complex.

It was with this as background that the annual budgetary discussions got underway. These had always been carried on in a very gentlemanly way in a Finance Committee composed of faculty, administrative, and trustee representatives. This year, however, things were different. Money was tight, and any extra funds added to one area of operations would have to be subtracted from another. Each staff member, fearing that his or her own ox might be gored, found some reason to oppose any major change from the previous year's expenditures. And, since over three-quarters of the budget went to salaries, more money allocated to new programs meant that less money would be available for salary increases. The faculty considered such raises to be essential, since the inflationary pressures that were making the college's budget tight were having a similar effect on their family budgets.

Although the faculty rejected the idea of a special College Transition Program, they were not insensitive to the needs of less fortunate students. They felt, however, that the remedial courses already available at Hillsdale were sufficient. Despite the fact that these courses returned less than 10% of their "graduates" to the educational mainstream — a figure typical of junior colleges in their state, incidentally, — they still believed that the college was doing all it should to remedy the deficiencies rooted in earlier school experiences. The teachers were joined in their opposition by the dean of students. He firmly believed that those community colleges that offered individual tutoring, child care facilities, job placement help, financial aid, and other special services were going way beyond their mandate. In this era of limited funds, he was convinced that every cent was needed to continue basic services like counseling, guidance, and student activities. Thus, he opposed the College Transition Program both on principle and on the practical basis of lack of funds. Merkens, representing the Board on the Finance Committee, pushed hard for the program but could garner no support.

Dr. Wilkinson tried to convince the Finance Committee of the critical need for initiating new occupational courses. He insisted that the college might well lose its accreditation if this were not done. Despite this, the other members remained adamantly opposed to the idea because of the increased costs involved. After a series of meetings failed to produce a solution, it was agreed, in the interests of harmony, to present a budget containing only one new feature: a scaled-down appropriation for adding two new occupational programs to the curriculum. Merkens was very displeased with the group's decision and vowed to plead his case before the full Board.

The proposed budget was presented to the Board at a study session on April 15, followed by a discussion at their regular meeting on May 3. Merkens told his fellow trustees that both a vastly expanded vocational program and the College Transition Program were essential and that other, less critical, items must be cut from the budget to make room for them. Lopez seconded this request. They were joined by an unexpected ally, Ralph Jones, vice-president of the bank in San Cristobal. His finger was on the economic pulse of the community and he had become convinced that better occupational training would benefit both the young people in the area and their potential employers. Although he wasn't too enthusiastic about the Transition Program, he was willing to join with any other trustees who would help get the vocational program into the budget. The "pros" thus had three votes — but the fourth was not forthcoming.

The other trustees voiced their satisfaction with the Finance Committee's proposal. Dr. Bertram Marshall, a retired professor from the state university, genuinely believed that a college should offer only transfer courses; he also tended, all things being equal, to go along with the faculty's recommendations. Jim Carpenter, a 55-year old realtor, had run for the Board to gain status in the eyes of his wife's family, all of whom were teachers; he too liked the idea of Hillsdale as a "college" rather than a "trade school." Mike Hultgren, also in his fifties, was an orchardist caught in the financial squeeze common to agriculturists on the edge of suburbia; he believed that the president should be given a free hand to run the college as long as he did it at the lowest possible cost to the taxpayers. The seventh trustee was Dr. Alfred Bugliotti, a local dentist; he was very proud of Hillsdale College, of its faculty and of its president, and would do anything within his power to help them provide the kind of educational program they thought best.

Before the budget could be officially adopted, state law required that a public hearing be held. It was scheduled for May 17. Although few people usually attended board meetings, the room was packed for the budget hearing. The Student Council argued in favor of the College Transition Program, as did the various politically-oriented student organizations. Representatives of the local minority communities were there to plead for it, also. The League of Women Voters had studied community college education that year; their work had led them to agree that major changes should be made in Hillsdale's program. Their final report drew some invidious comparisons between the proportion of the population taking courses at Hillsdale and that enrolled at other colleges in the state. They concluded that the relatively low attendance at Hillsdale was due in great part to the lack of vocational opportunities and the dearth of special help for disadvantaged students. The Business and Industry Club of San Cristobal sent a spokesman to urge expanded technical training. A retired man begged the Board to consider the plight of those living on fixed incomes when considering expensive new programs. He was informed — if not necessarily convinced — that whatever action the Board took, there could be no tax increase. Since the college was already levying as high a rate as the law permitted, further increases could be authorized only by a vote of the people. Since similar tax increase elections were failing regularly throughout the state, there was not the remotest possibility that the Hillsdale trustees would seek an increase.

At the close of the public segment of the meeting, Dr. Wilkinson and the staff reiterated their support for the budget as recommended. Board reaction indicated that their opinions had not changed since the previous meeting. Marshall moved adoption of the budget. Carpenter seconded, and it was passed by a 4-3 vote, with Merkens, Lopez, and Jones dissenting.

The crowd's displeasure with this action was clear, but they filed from the room in an orderly fashion. For the next hour they could be heard milling around in the corridor outside. Unbeknownst to the trustees, this milling was to good purpose and would eventuate in the ouster of two of their number. They were deciding to meet the following week to seek ways of getting Hillsdale to move in the areas of concern to them.

This first meeting was well attended. Representatives from all the interested student groups were present, as well as spokesmen for the Mexican-American, Asian, and black organizations in the area. The County Employers' Association sent an observer, as did the Business and Industry Club. Although the League of Women Voters could not participate officially, several study group members chose to do so as individuals. The Management Club from the assembly plant was represented. Several teachers from Hillsdale, emboldened by this show of public support, came out of the closet and announced their support of the proposed changes.

After much discussion, those present decided that the one thing they had in common was a desire to get Hillsdale moving. They therefore decided to call themselves the "Coalition Interested in Change at Hillsdale" or "CICH," which formed an acceptable — if somewhat less than ideal — acronym. Further discussion led to the conclusion that the only way to change Hillsdale was to change the Board of Trustees. Plans were duly made to challenge some of the incumbents at the next election, scheduled for late October. Three seats would be up for grabs at that time, one belonging to Ralph Jones and the other two to supporters of the *status quo*. CICH members realized that they had a hard task before them if they expected to unseat incumbents, since no incumbent had ever been defeated when seeking re-election to the Hillsdale Board. They decided to lay their plans over the summer and move into action immediately after Labor Day. The first order of business, of course, was to find suitable candidates. A committee was appointed to gather names and return two weeks hence with their recommendations.

Committee members came up with a list of five potential candidates to challenge Carpenter and Bugliotti, whose seats were at stake. In sounding out their choices, they found that one was unwilling to run for family and business reasons, one was reluctant to go through the trauma of campaigning, one was on the fence, and two were enthusiastic when they learned that CICH volunteers would plan and run their campaigns. With this information in hand, the committee returned to the group and received its blessing for their two top choices: Ted Nakamura, a 30-year old lawyer, himself a graduate of Hillsdale, and Mrs. Yvonne Perkins, active community worker and former League of Women Voters' president. They both accepted and CICH began to plan for the fall campaign.

At this point CICH went public with its plans. The idea was to scare off other potential candidates and to attract help from all those who shared its goals. As the October election approached, Jim Carpenter decided to drop out rather than face the stiff competition he expected from Ted Nakamura. He had never before been opposed when running for office and did not have the stomach to wage an all-out campaign. Dr. Bugliotti, however, was most anxious to retain his seat and laid plans for an aggressive campaign. Jones was also up for election, but he faced only token opposition.

The contest between Mrs. Perkins and Dr. Bugliotti was intense and hard-fought. They were both well known in the community, both had many fine attributes. Mrs. Perkins, of course, had CICH behind her to raise money and organize her campaign. She also had many willing workers among the women she had gotten to know in other civic activities. The Women's Political Movement, a relatively new group organized specifically to promote women in public office, came to her aid. Appalled at the dearth of women on school boards in general and on the Hillsdale board in particular, they brought dedicated womanpower and political expertise to the effort. Another splinter group from the Hillsdale faculty appeared: composed mainly of women, it too felt that the all-male Board was an anachronism that should not be perpetuated. Since her children were all teenagers, Mrs. Perkins had plenty of time to devote to campaigning. Although she did not actually walk precincts, she attended enough coffees and organization meetings to meet many of her constituents. Her advisers considered this personal contact to be essential for a woman candidate, who must usually be seen to be believed.

Dr. Bugliotti, on the other hand, had the advantage of incumbency and of the strong support of the Hillsdale faculty. Although the latter decided against coming out officially in his favor, they worked hard in the background raising money, sponsoring coffees, and getting endorsements. There was on campus a small but active chapter of the American Federation of Teachers. Through their connections with other segments of organized labor in the Hillsdale area, they were able to round up considerable union support — both in money and in endorsements — for Dr. Bugliotti. His colleagues in the health professions, pleased to have one of their number on the college board, contributed their names and their dollars to his campaign. Also out working for him were the members of the local service club in which he had been active for many years. In the Bugliotti camp too were the long-time landowners; they had accepted the college grudgingly and certainly did not want it to expand in any way. Many retired people shared this fear that the proposed changes would inevitably bring higher taxes. These two groups plus a few businessmen formed the backbone of the highly vocal, but not too well-respected, Taxpayers' United Association, which came out for Bugliotti.

The race was close right up to the end. The Perkins' forces were delighted when the local newspaper rated the candidates as equally capable; since the editor usually sided with incumbents, his neutrality was considered a major victor. On election day, few felt they could predict the outcome with any certainty. It was not until late on election evening that a pattern began to emerge. When over half the votes were counted, Mrs. Perkins began slowly but surely to pull away from her opponent. The final tally showed that her margin of victory was a mere 5% of the votes cast. Almost 30% of the voters had gone to the polls — a high turnout for a school election.

Mr. Nakamura, Mrs. Perkins and their three like-minded colleagues on the Board felt that they had a clear — if not exactly overwhelming — mandate from the electorate. The majority of those who cared enough to vote apparently did want some changes to be made at Hillsdale. Mrs. Perkins felt a strong obligation to CICH and to the friends who had worked so hard for her election. Her feeling of indebtedness stemmed not from the great sums of money they had donated but from the time and effort they had put into helping her. And, of course, she had initially agreed to run because of a personal commitment to instituting a College Transition Program and expanding vocational opportunities.

The new Board was officially seated on January 2. Their immediate problem was to decide how to encourage and, if necessary, to force the college staff to make the desired changes. Due to the pre-election publicity, there was no question in anybody's mind as to the Board's desires. A few of the faculty had favored the new approach for a long time; others had come around during the campaign; but a majority still remained unconvinced. The Board recognized that it had to do three things to be sure the will of the people was carried out: to adopt policies embodying the new philosophy, to allocate monies for the new programs, and to employ personnel to see that they were spent in an effective manner. The first was easiest, and was accomplished within the month. A new budget could not be adopted in the middle of the school year, however, so they would have to wait until spring to divert substantial sums to the new programs. In the interim, they would "find" a few unspent dollars in the nooks and crannies of the current budget to get things off the ground.

They also began to gear up the administrative staff to implement the new policies. After several long private sessions, they announced that the  dean of students  would be reassigned as of July 1 to the newly created position of Grants and Development Director. This seemed an appropriate switch, since he worked well with the faculty and all agreed on the need for such a position. The real reason, of course, was that he had lost the confidence of a large segment of the student body and of the Board through his opposition to the College Transition Program. Some said that he was the sacrificial lamb to show that the Board meant business, but others recognized that he was simply paying the penalty for getting out of step with the times. The director of vocational education, by contrast, was in seventh heaven: he was now urged to do all the things he had been dreaming of for the past decade! He dusted off some proposals which had earlier been described as empire-building and found that they were now hailed as visionary. He, at least, was more than ready to move as soon as the budgetary constraints could be removed.

The major question in most people's minds was the sincerity of Dr. Wilkinson's conversion to the "New Look." His previous stand had been dictated by the wishes of his Board and had the enthusiastic approval of the faculty. Thus some felt that he had had little choice in the matter. Others, however, criticized him for not exercising the leadership expected of a professional educator. Dr. Bugliotti's backers were particularly bitter that Wilkinson had not been foresighted enough to save his most loyal supporter from defeat at the polls. Marshall and Hultgren were somewhat annoyed with him for the same reason, but they realized that they, too, were to blame for failing to assess public opinion accurately. Lopez and Jones also had ambivalent feelings toward the president, feeling that he was a good administrator even if his crystal ball was rather cloudy. Mrs. Perkins and Nakamura were reluctant to take the lead in suggesting that Wilkinson be ousted since they were so new to the Board. Also, he had made himself personally most agreeable to them during the campaign and had been helpful in supplying whatever background information or services they requested. Only Merkens was certain that Wilkinson would have to go, but he hesitated to go out on a limb without knowing the feelings of his colleagues. Most of all he would have liked to make some wholesale changes in the faculty, who, he felt, were unsympathetic to the needs of non-WASP students. Since the Board was precluded by state law from firing tenured faculty, the only personnel changes that it could make were in the administrative staff. The first step had already been taken by the reassignment of the dean of students. Merkens felt that in order to really change the overall direction of the college it would be necessary, at the very least, to replace Dr. Wilkinson. Not wishing to risk rebuff from his fellow trustees, however, he decided to keep his thoughts to himself for the time being.

Dr. Wilkinson was not insensitive to the thinking of his Board. In fact, he had seen the handwriting on the wall on election night when the voters rejected the continuation of the *status quo* at Hillsdale. He made it known to his professional colleagues that he was actively looking for a new job, giving the excuse that

13 years was much too long for an administrator to stay in any one place. With the proliferation of community colleges across the country, the demand for experienced administrators was high. As expected, Dr. Wilkinson did not have long to wait: within a few months he had offers from two eastern communities to become their college's founding president. One of them closely resembled the Hillsdale area of fifteen years earlier, and it was there that Dr. Wilkinson decided to go.

During the spring budgetary discussions the Board assigned top priority to the expansion of vocational courses and the initiation of the College Transition Program. Although the amount of discretionary funds was limited, it was their decision that even traditional programs would have to be cut back or eliminated to make room for the new ones. Thus, the budget adopted in June reflected the changes promised in the previous year's election campaign. It was about this time that Dr. Wilkinson announced his impending resignation. The Board thus found itself in the enviable position of being able to pick a leader for the college who would enthusiastically promote its new approach to community education. The position of dean of students was purposely left unfilled so that its new occupant would be in tune with the thinking of both the new Board majority and the new president.

Thus, within one short year, Hillsdale College changed from an institution mired down in the past to one that was ready and anxious to enter the future. The forces for change, of course, had been building for some time. But it was just at this time that the balance tipped, that motion triumphed over inertia. Appropriately — since Hillsdale is a locally controlled college — the decision was made by the local residents. Forces on the outside — the accrediting agency, the state Coordinating Council, the federal government — contributed also, as did the minority of faculty members and administrators who recognized the need for change. But the real impetus came from the community: from those who persuaded Raul Lopez that Hillsdale was not giving his fellow Mexican-Americans a fair shake, from those who convinced Ralph Jones that more vocational courses would be beneficial for all, and, finally, in the most time-honored democratic manner, from those who elected both of them plus Merkens, Nakamura, and Mrs. Perkins to the Board of Trustees of Hillsdale College.

# CHAPTER 6
# The Board of Trustees: Membership and Performance

According to legend, Mark Twain once remarked, "First God practiced on idiots, then he created school boards." A superintendent more recently described his county board as composed of one common crook, one alcoholic, and one total illiterate, "a bunch of peanut politicians — so low they could walk under a snake's belly."[1] Just a few years ago John Kenneth Galbraith called the governing board of the American university "an anachronism . . . but not yet a harmless anachronism . . . it remains a barrier to rational progress."[2] And another critic, speaking of college and university boards, believes that "Trustees fall short of their responsibilities with sufficient frequency that they lend considerable strength to the view that . . . they should be gotten rid of altogether."[3]

Fortunately, none of these derogatory comments was aimed directly at community college trustees. Indeed, there is some evidence that they may rank relatively high in the esteem of their fellow men. In 1970 some 200 community college presidents were asked to rate the performance of their boards: they considered slightly more than 50 percent "excellent," another 20 percent "good," and only 3 percent clearly "bad."[4] This rosy picture must be viewed with a certain amount of suspicion, however, since the respondents may have felt that their boards had proven their competency merely by their wise choice of presidents. A more impartial source, the Carnegie Commission on Higher Education, studied all aspects of the control of colleges and universities. They recommended "the preservation (or creation) of strong and independent boards of trustees with basic responsibility for the welfare of institutions of higher education."[5]

Whatever the track record of boards of trustees, there seems to be one overriding reason why they are here to stay — no one has found a better way to govern educational institutions. As Winston Churchill once said of the system of government of which school boards are one small part: "No one pretends that democracy is perfect or all-wise; indeed, it has been said that democracy is the worst form of government except all those other forms that have been tried from time to time."[6] Discussion thus centers not on whether or not boards of trustees should be continued but rather on how they can be made to function most effectively.

### Who are the Trustees?

A recent study by Morton Rauh of some 261 trustees in 67 public community colleges has provided much-needed data on board members. The following picture of today's trustee emerges from his survey:

| Sex | | Age | |
|---|---|---|---|
| Male | 84% | Under 40 | 12% |
| **Race** | | 40-49 | 26% |
| Caucasian | 95% | 50-59 | 36% |
| Negro | 2% | 60-69 | 19% |
| **Formal Education** | | 70 or over | 7% |
| Not H.S. Graduate | 2% | **Income** | |
| H.S. Graduate | 5% | Less than $6,000 | 3% |
| Some College | 23% | $6,000 – $10,000 | 10% |
| B.A., B.S. | 26% | $10,000 – $20,000 | 30% |
| Graduate School | 10% | $20,000 – $30,000 | 25% |
| Advanced Degrees | 31% | $30,000 – $50,000 | 20% |
| | | Over $50,000 | 10% |

**Occupation**
Executive (Manufacturing, Bank, Business, Insurance,
   Foundation)           36%

| | | |
|---|---|---|
| Professional (Lawyer, M.D., Dentist, Architect, Clergy-man, Accountant, Consultant, Educator, Journalist) | | 33% |
| Farmer | | 9% |
| Government (Elected Official, Administrator) | | 8% |
| Community Volunteer | | 4% |

**Religious Affiliation**

| | |
|---|---|
| Protestant | 77% |
| Catholic | 11% |
| Jewish | 7% |
| No Formal | 4% |

| **Political Party Preference** | | **Political Ideology** | |
|---|---|---|---|
| Republican | 52% | Conservative | 25% |
| Democratic | 39% | Moderate | 60% |
| Other | 5% | Liberal | 13%[7] |

The typical community college trustee thus appears to be a white, Protestant, male college graduate, over 50 years old, who earns more than $20,000 a year as an executive or professional man. Other studies on a more limited basis – in various states, for example – have produced almost identical statistics.

Interestingly, these figures have held almost constant over the past half-century, if we consider public school trustees as a whole. (Since community colleges have so little recorded history of their own, some of the data presented here comes from studies of trustees at other levels of the educational system.) Dr. George Counts broke ground almost 50 years ago with a pioneering study of the social composition of school boards. He found that in communities of 2,500 or more the schools were securely in the hands of upper-income groups, regardless of the socioeconomic makeup of the populace. Two-thirds of the trustees were either proprietors, professional men, or managers, while a mere 8 percent were industrial workers. Housewives had made some inroads by the 1920's, but trustees felt that one female member per board was adequate.[8]

Although the situation has apparently remained almost static since then, there are some indications that the pace of change may be accelerating. In a follow-up to Rauh's study, it was found that in one year 7 percent of the community college boards had added blacks, 10 percent had increased the number of women, nearly one-quarter had added members under 40 (exclusive of students), 12 percent had more people whose occupations were in the creative arts, and 10 percent had added educators employed by institutions other than the college on whose board they serve.[9]

### Background-Performance Relationship

But why go into so much detail about the private lives of trustees? After all, what matters to their constituents is how they feel about community college matters, not where they go to church or what income-tax bracket they're in. If they are people of integrity and are in tune with the values, the needs, and the aspirations of the community, what matters their sex or age? The presumption, of course, is that trustees' thinking and voting are determined by their personal characteristics and economic status.

This thesis has come under increasing attack in recent studies. We all know from personal experience that two people who look identical on paper can hold diametrically opposed views on social and political issues. Who has not witnessed a knock-down, drag-out argument between two blue-collar, Catholic, male workers over preferential hiring for minorities? Or a less-than-lady-like discussion between two upper-class white matrons over the desirability of welfare? Even sex is not a certain predictor of voting patterns: when the city council in a San Francisco suburb voted to refuse the use of its public ballpark for Little League games unless girls were allowed to play, the lone woman member of the council dissented. She opposed the proposal because she felt that girls should not engage in sports like baseball. And on the national level, there have been many well-known public figures — Franklin Delano Roosevelt is a prime example — whose actions were so abhorrent to their peers that they were called traitors to their class, which had apparently influenced their thinking only slightly if at all.

Obviously, no valid generalization can be drawn from these incidents. But several serious research studies have looked closely at the relationship between the social status of trustees and their role performance. One of these asked public school superintendents to categorize the motivations of their trustees as "good" (in the office for the purpose of civic service) or "bad" (in office to serve their own ends or those of a special-interest group). The attempt was then made to find the relationship, if any, between motivation and personal and socioeconomic characteristics. The results indicated little relationship between motivation and the occupation, education, sex, marital status, or income of the trustees surveyed. They were, however, considerably more likely to fall into the "good" category if they had children, were older (at least up to 65), had served for some time on the board, or sent some of their children to private schools![10]

Another study attempted to identify those factors which affected the "educational progressivism" of trustees. The only related characteristic turned out to be amount of education; none of the others tested — income, religion, age — seemed to be relevant.[11] These findings are in accord with the conclusion of other researchers that there is little if any relationship between trustees' socioeconomic beliefs and their attitudes toward the improvement of education. They suggest, in fact, that a negative correlation might exist, that relatively higher educational and occupational levels might be associated with more liberal attitudes toward the educational function.[12]

A study of Oregon trustees found that their values with respect to education could not even be accurately predicted on the basis of their known political values.[13] Rauh also found that "political leaning is not the most reliable indicator of position on educational issues."[14] As an example, when the trustees in his study were queried as to the characteristics they thought board members should have, over 70 percent agreed that one of the most important was "impatience with the *status quo*" — a rather startling attitude, considering that over 85 percent labeled themselves as moderate or conservative in political outlook.[15]

The most recent work in this field was done by Rodney Hartnett as a follow-up to Rauh's study of trusteeship in higher education. He attempted to correlate trustees' attitudes towards academic freedom and democratic governance of the college with their personal and demographic characteristics. He contrasted businessmen with non-businessmen and found the latter to be more liberal. But when trustees were asked who they felt should be served by higher education, there were no consistent differences among occupational groups. Women and the better educated tended to be more liberal on the academic freedom and governance issues, but neither the income nor the political party affiliation of community college trustees showed a distinct correlation.[16] Although hardly conclusive, this study is a welcome step in the direction of ascertaining the influence of trustees' characteristics on their performance.

One author sums up all these results by stating that "the findings of these studies have not borne out the assumption that the attitudes or behavior of members are unambiguously related to their social characteristics."[17]

It may well be that those trustees who succeed in getting elected do so because their values transcend those of any one class or interest group. In order to garner sufficient votes, their appeal must be to a broad spectrum of the populace. One author suggests that the social structure in which local school boards are embedded in some way screens or nullifies the expected effects of social background on attitudes.  He concludes that trustees apparently do try to represent the *entire* community, regardless of their own particular background or beliefs.[18]

### Other Influences on Trustee Performance

There are many explanations for the apparent lack of congruence between trustees' characteristics and their educational outlook. Only one of the surveys quoted, for example, attempts to probe their reasons for seeking office. This is not surprising, since trustees themselves — let alone outside observers — often do not understand their real motives for wanting to be a school board member. Community college boards are full of people officially categorized as doctors, housewives, and salesmen who became trustees for reasons totally unrelated to their occupations or political beliefs. A recent study found that an amazingly large number of board members have close personal ties with the field of education: 60 percent of those surveyed had at least one relative in school work, over half had one or both parents or a spouse so employed, and 20 percent had themselves held jobs in education![19] Men  with less education than their colleagues run for the board to gain respectability in the eyes of the world; women whose teacher-fathers chafed under the rule of a dictatorial school board seek belated redress of grievances; and members of both sexes enter the fray at the behest of relatives and friends in the teaching profession. Since the strings are here being pulled by unseen hands, their actions as trustees cannot be predicted from any set of characteristics visible to the inquiring researcher or the general public.

One observer divides trustees into five broad types according to motivation: Clients (they protect the student), Guardians (they protect the taxpayer's dollar), Benefactors (they offer their services out of a sense of *noblesse oblige*), Politicians (they are en route to higher office), and Mavericks (even they sometimes don't seem to know why they are there).[20] Whatever their backgrounds, each of these "types" clearly marches to the music of a different drummer.

Effective performance on the part of trustees is also dependent upon personality characteristics. Although they are not required to be absolute paragons, good trustees do need to have a high proportion of admirable traits. One study indicates that the most important of these — at least as seen by fellow Board members — are good judgment, strong convictions that stand up against pressure, the ability to speak well, knowledge of the schools and the board's functions, open-mindedness, a willingness to listen, intelligence, and fairness.[21] One writer describes an ideal trustee as follows: "Besides a devotion to public education . . . he should have more than average ability, a capacity for understanding his fellow man in spite of differences of opinion, an independent mind but not a belligerent nature . . . and willingness to spend untold quantities of time and energy for no compensation beyond the satisfaction of doing public service. As if all that were not enough, it is usually suggested that he have a sense of humor."[22] Although these personal and behavioral characteristics are difficult to measure — especially for the voting public during a campaign — their effect on trustee performance is undisputed.

### Improving Trustee Performance

One of the more common criticisms of trustees is that they do not devote enough time to their board duties. The difficulty lies in deciding how much is enough; since the job itself is so ill-defined, it is almost impossible for even the most conscientious trustees to know if they are doing too little or too much. According to Rauh's study, the median number of hours per year spent by community college trustees on college activities — board meetings, committees, *ad hoc* meetings, speeches, conferences with college personnel — comes to 82, or an average of less than two hours per week.[23] Trustees receive conflicting advice as to how much time they should invest: a few presidents welcome "professional" trustees, but most are wary of retired admirals, housewives with grown children, and airline pilots with free daytime hours; some faculty enjoy the attention of board members, while others consider them a nuisance; and members of the community are practically unanimous in preferring trustees who have lots of time for college activities. Voters have long reacted favorably to candidates who promise that, if elected, they will "devote full-time to the job of trustee." Since the power to choose board members rests in the hands of the public, their desire for more trustee involvement will probably prevail.

One thing that can be said with assurance is that trusteeship takes more time now than it did in the past and will take still more in the future. The community colleges are becoming more and more complex, the populations they serve are larger and more heterogeneous, and their needs are more difficult to ascertain and fulfill. More citizens are demanding the right to participate in the decision-making process, to work with those who have power rather than with their representatives. No longer can angry constituents be foisted off onto an assistant dean; now they demand the right to take their case directly to the top. Participatory democracy takes time — on the part of elected officials as well as of interested citizens.

The community colleges are not unique in demanding more and more time on the part of their governing officials. There was a time when even state legislators were farmers, lawyers, and merchants who took a few days or weeks from their regular work to attend to the state's business. Today, in the larger states at least, their jobs have become almost year-round; and the changeover from citizen-lawmaker to professional legislator is well underway. The time required by many local offices too has escalated to the point where they are looked upon as at least part-time occupations. Community college boards, especially those with responsibility for several campuses, are now beginning to follow in their footsteps.

A closely related topic is salary. As long as trustees are putting in but a few hours a week, their ability to earn a living is unimpaired. But once board duties start to make massive inroads on their time, the question of compensation arises. Attendance at state and national meetings, for example, requires trustees to be away from their regular jobs for several days at a time. Some college activities — meetings with staff and students, discussions with public officials — can only be accomplished during working hours. When these demands become so great that the average citizen cannot meet them and do justice to a full-time job as well, payment becomes mandatory. The only alternative is for time-consuming elective positions to become the exclusive province of the rich and the retired. Even where board responsibilities are relatively light, lower-income citizens are sometimes excluded from membership because of the out-of-pocket expenses involved. Small stipends are of help in covering costs of transportation, babysitting, and an occasional luncheon meeting, even though they do not solve the problem of excessive time away from the job. Here again the situation is analogous to that of other public officials, both state and local: some states are now paying living wages to their legislators, and city councilmen, county supervisors, and trustees in large school districts are likely to receive stipends commensurate with the amount of time devoted to their office.

Many observers deplore this development, feeling that salaries lead people to run for office for monetary reasons rather than from a desire to be of service. They point to the many hours given by citizens to other unpaid activities — churches, Little League, charities — and hold that there are plenty of people from all walks of life who would be delighted to do the same for their community colleges. Nonetheless, the trend seems to be for community college trustees to join the growing ranks of state and local officials who are paid for their services.

Trustees themselves feel that the lack of information is the greatest deterrent to effective performance. In a recent survey some 118 presidents of community college boards were asked how the college president could be of most help to them. Their response was nearly unanimous: they wanted him or her to give them information — concisely, thoroughly, and honestly.[24] This item was far ahead of anything else on their list. An earlier study of high school trustees yielded similar results: more of the respondents were dissatisfied with the level of information they received than with any other factor affecting board functioning.[25] There is no doubt that trustees, like computers, cannot do an adequate job with inadequate information; "garbage in, garbage out," is, unfortunately, true for both.

The first question that comes to mind is "How much information is needed?" Since information is not readily quantifiable, rules-of-thumb are hard to come by. The optimum amount can only be determined by discussion between the board and staff of each college. It may vary widely even within a single board: some members are frustrated by too little information, others overwhelmed by too much. Staff are disappointed if their carefully prepared reports go unread. Probably the best approach is to make available as much information as the most conscientious trustee is willing to absorb. Of equal importance is the form in which information is presented: busy trustees are much more likely to read and understand a single-page summary than a stack of detailed material.

And from whom should the board get its information? Traditionally, all input to trustees has been filtered through the college president. There are still some good reasons for this: screening out trivia and irrelevancies, collating data from various sources to present a balanced view, and the like. But it also means that one individual's stamp is put on every bit of data that reaches trustees. Some presidents, taking a cue from the business world, use their power as gatekeeper to manipulate the thinking of their board. "Corporate managers expend considerable effort to protect their domain from prying eyes. Secrecy is a passion in large corporations because corporate managers understand better than anyone else that controlling information is the key to exercising power."[26] Even if presidents are not consciously trying to limit or distort the information they pass on to their board, the flavor of the original is lost en route. Trustees can prevent this by making sure they receive input directly from many sources: citizens' committees, student and faculty representatives, and college publications are among the many excellent ones available. In return, they should use all this information judiciously and share with the president and staff pertinent data received from sources of their own. Assuring an adequate flow of information to the board should be a cooperative venture involving all elements of the college community and must be assigned a high priority within each institution. Some feel, however, that even this is bound to fail, that as long as trustees are dependent on the college staff alone, they will never get the quality and quantity of information they need. They maintain that ultimately boards of trustees — especially those responsible for many colleges — will have to hire research staffs of their own.

The possibilities for improving board performance in other ways are almost endless, limited only by the time, the commitment, and the imagination of both trustees and staff. They range from nuts-and-bolts activities like visiting other colleges, attending workshops, and hiring consultants to proposals for helping trustees develop the attitudes, abilities, and skills needed to deal with whatever community college problems arise. Trustees' interest in participating in these "upgrading" activities is high. They are becoming increasingly active in regional and state community college affairs. Within the past few years, trustees have taken on a greatly expanded role within the American Association of Community and Junior Colleges and have formed a new organization, the Association of Community College Trustees, to deal specifically with the problems of community college trusteeship.

### Diversifying Membership of Boards of Trustees

Despite the evidence that trustees' performance cannot be predicted from their personal or social characteristics — or perhaps because it is not widely known — community college boards are frequently criticized for the lack of diversity in their membership. The assumption is that their homogeneity renders them incapable of representing the many different segments of the community. One author argues that "Although to infer attitudes and behaviors from the social origins and positions of public officials is a well-established fallacy, social characteristics are

important in at least three aspects. First, the inclusion or exclusion
of certain strata has great symbolic value . . . Second, it is un-
doubtedly true that some public leaders do serve their class interests ... Finally, it seems undeniable that certain perspectives or
*Weltanshauung* are inevitably underrepresented on governing
boards by virtue of their status bias."[27] The suggestion has been
made that trustees should take it upon themselves to remedy
this inequity: they should, if necessary, "step down so that they
can be replaced by members of unrepresented groups."[28] Others
feel that some mechanism should be devised to assure seats on
community college boards for the major subgroups in
the electorate.

Still others are horrified at these suggestions, considering them
a dangerous circumvention of the electoral process. They fear that
assigning seats to special groups would be opening Pandora's box,
that the list of groups claiming special consideration would be
endless and equity impossible to attain. They cite the difficulty
of dividing up the available slots and finding suitable candidates
to fill them. Boards would either have to be large enough to seat
representatives from every community subgroup — and expand-
able as new ones are identified — or members would have to possess a specific combination of characteristics. One might have to
be old, Protestant, female, poor, and a resident of the southern
part of the district, while another should live in the central
area and be a young, Spanish-speaking, blue-collar alumnus —
clearly statistical abstractions rather than warm bodies. And even
if these prototypes are uncovered, there is no guarantee that their
thinking about community colleges would coincide with that
of others in their sex, age, or economic bracket.

There is also the concern that trustees chosen by subgroups
would feel a primary responsibility to the electing constituency
rather than to the total college and community. This would
undermine the traditional role of the board as an impartial
steward, as the guardian of the public interest. In cases of conflict
between the interests of a subgroup and that of the community
as a whole, trustees must be free to give priority to the latter.[29]
Thus, many fear that election by special interest groups would
in the long run prove more deleterious than the currently skewed
composition of boards of trustees. Morris Keaton sums up this

controversy by pointing out that "Those who protect the public interest in governing need not be altogether typical of the public they protect. The constituencies should have effective advocacy before, and response from, the board; they need not be, and cannot always be, equally well represented on the board."[30]

Even those who oppose guaranteeing board seats to special interest groups agree that the *opportunity* for membership should be equally open to all citizens. Although many trustees can and do represent all segments of the community regardless of their own background, the fact remains that people from certain racial, ethnic, and economic groups are usually excluded from membership. The statistics presented earlier prove beyond a doubt that community college boards are not mirror images of their constituencies. Nor, for that matter, are most of our democratically elected governing bodies. The most recent figures on the United States Congress, for example, show that the average age of its 535 members is 54.1 years, only 14 of them are women and 13 black, and well over half are lawyers by profession – hardly a composite portrait of the American people.[31] This, then, is a problem of democracy rather than of the community colleges, and its solution must be sought in the reform of the democratic process.

Constitutionally, all citizens have an equal chance to be elected to office. In actual practice, this opportunity seems to be monopolized by upper-class white males. Invisible barriers apparently keep the poor, the dark of skin, and the female out of this charmed circle. Some of these barriers are so deeply imbedded in our social structure that they can only be eradicated on a long-term basis. Others, however, are relatively easy to identify and to eliminate, requiring only the widespread adoption of known techniques. The two major obstacles in this category – both of which are relevant to potential community college trustees – are lack of know-how and lack of money.

To the uninitiated, the organization of a campaign is a complete mystery, while to the veteran political worker it is a simple, open-and-shut proposition. The details vary from campaign to campaign, but the underlying principles remain the same. What is needed is to introduce the political novice – particularly if he or she is from a social or ethnic group which lacks a tradition of political participation — to those who know how to run successful campaigns. Political parties have long filled this function, but only a tiny percentage of trustee elections are partisan. Actually, teachers' organizations, for example, sometimes have a political arm whose function is to help friendly candidates. And sometimes there are citizens' caucuses, groups of people without any axes to grind, who band together to seek out good candidates and work for their election. They raise money, plot strategy, arrange for publicity, set up meetings — in short, do what is necessary to win election in their particular community. They are not invariably successful, but their rate is high by any standards. Caucuses can be equally effective in areas where trustees are appointed; the strategy then is to bring pressure to bear on the appointing authority to choose a community-supported candidate. Remember that the governor, who usually makes these appointments, is ultimately responsible to the electorate and therefore anxious to remain in its good graces.

The other ingredient necessary for success at the polls is money. To be sure, there are areas in which it is considered neither necessary nor appropriate to spend much money to gain election to the community college board. But in many of the large areas served by community colleges the necessary name recognition can only be attained through extensive use of newspapers, radio, television, home mailings, and the like — a very expensive proposition. The need for such heavy expenditures is particularly acute for the outsider trying to break into the ranks of the incumbents or of the traditional community leadership. This problem is widely recognized at all levels of government, and many schemes are afoot to do something about it. Most prominent among them are government financing of campaigns, public disclosure of contributions, and the imposition of expenditure limits.

### Faculty-Administrative Representation on Boards of Trustees

Other critics of community college boards as now constituted advocate setting aside seats for faculty and administrators. Their reasons are twofold: they feel that those most closely associated with the college should share in the decision-making power and that a body of laymen cannot possess the expertise needed to run today's complex institutions.A precedent does exist for including staff on boards: the presidents of most four-year colleges and universities have traditionally been granted membership on their own boards, and institutions sponsored by religious denominations have often included faculty as well. One major difference between these boards and those of most community colleges is size: the latter average about nine members, the former several times this number. Thus they can assign one or more seats to staff without substantially tipping the balance of power away from the lay membership. In Canadian community colleges the college president, a college faculty member, and a college student each hold voting rights on a typical nine-member board.

Opponents of this approach for community colleges argue that it violates one of the basic premises of democratic government, that all social institutions should be under lay control. If teachers and administrators sit on the governing board of their own colleges, why not include city managers and firemen on the city councils they serve? Or turn over a substantial proportion of the seats in the House of Representatives to the generals, diplomats, and civil servants they hire to carry out their will? Although all of these legislative units are dependent on professionals to execute their mandates, they do not give them voting power in the policy-making body itself.

Supporters of the present system claim that professionals already exercise far too much influence on college matters because of the lay trustee's reluctance to challenge their supposed expertise. They would like to see lay control strengthened, not further eroded. They argue that final decisions should be left to the "generalists," that the ideas of the educator should prevail only if they can also win the approval of the layman; this builds checks and balances into the system.[32] The feeling runs very deep that common men's collective wisdom, as voiced through elective bodies, is at least as valid as that of the experts. In other words, Clemenceau's famous statement about war, that it is "too important an endeavor to be left solely to the generals" — applies equally to education.[33] The argument against setting aside board seats for community subgroups applies equally to faculty: if the board is to act in the general public interest, then its members should not be elected as the spokesmen of any special group.

Community college faculty members, of course, have the same

opportunity as other citizens to help elect or influence the appointment of sympathetic trustees. The teaching profession as a
whole has barely begun to flex its political muscle, but it is
learning fast. There are now almost three million classroom
teachers and other educational professionals on the public payroll.
Thus educators and their families now account for a larger segment of our population than the historically powerful farm bloc.
Moreover, they are becoming as well organized as agriculture,
with all that such capability portends in terms of political
influence.[34] According to one state official, teachers were by far
the biggest contributors to New York State legislative campaigns
last year, adding over $500,000 to candidates' coffers. California
teachers recently used $100,000 specifically to elect 152 local
school board candidates; of the 258 candidates they supported,
49 were educators. New York City's United Federation of
Teachers has proved that it can put up its own candidates and win
at least half the time in neighborhood school board contests.
Utah's teachers, who ten years ago were first to organize for political action, have elected 22 educators to their 104-member state
legislature; they often step in and run campaigns in addition to
making financial contributions to favored candidates.[35] Clearly
the ballot box is one potential route to power for community
college staff members.

### Student Representation on Boards

Many observers favor including students on community college
boards since they, most of all, bear the brunt of the board's
actions. Or, put more positively, those who are most strongly
affected by the board's decisions should share in making them.
Students in community colleges — where the age range is total
and the average is rising each year — are obviously mature and
experienced enough to have a say in planning their own education.

Opponents of guaranteeing board membership to students do
not deny this. They hold, however, that since almost all students
are now fully franchised members of the community, they should
seek power at the polls along with other citizens. If students care
enough to unite, their voting power will be irresistible. At DeAnza
College in Cupertino, California, for example, some 18,000
different people took courses for credit in 1970. At the next

trustee election — a hotly contested affair, featuring two incumbents and several challengers competing for three seats — less than 16,000 residents of the area actually went to the polls.[36] If the students at DeAnza had united behind a slate of candidates, they could easily have swept the election.

There is little merit in having student members of a board of trustees who do not represent the thinking of their peers. Thus, any valid plan for including students would have to be based on an elective system of some kind; since this system already exists in the many community colleges governed by elected trustees, students can find their way to office via the established route. Indeed, in the first year after the franchise was extended to 18-year-olds, several students were elected to community college boards. This trend can be expected to accelerate as students become more aware of their latent political strength. Those colleges with appointed boards will also find that officials charged with this responsibility are well aware of the voting power of students and anxious to cultivate their support by appointing them to boards of trustees.

### Alternatives to Faculty and Student Representation

Although wide differences of opinion exist as to the best solutions, there is general agreement that community colleges must strive to become more responsive to the needs of all those involved in the undertaking. Even those who reject the idea of guaranteeing board membership to faculty and students feel that they should be given more opportunity to participate in the internal governance system of the college. Most institutions have established specific channels — All-College Councils, Presidents' Advisory Committees, College Cabinets — whereby students and faculty can influence policy. All those potentially affected by a decision are consulted before the president recommends action to the board. If any segment of the college constituency does not agree with the president's recommendation, its representatives have the opportunity to appear before the board at an open meeting to plead their case. On some boards a faculty representative and/or a student representative sit with the board as nonvoting members and can directly express their constituents' views on any matter before a vote is taken. If trustees do not agree with their views and if they feel strongly enough about this rejection, they can take their case to the voters at the next election. More will be said about the internal governance of community colleges later; suffice it to say, that it is possible for faculty, administrators, and students to exercise a powerful influence on the board of trustees without ever being official members of that body.

## Conclusion

Recent surveys provide an excellent picture of the personal and social characteristics of community college trustees. Little effort, however, has been made to relate these characteristics to trustees' performance in office. Critics assail community college boards for their lack of diversity and of professional expertise, recommending that seats be made available to faculty, administrators, students, and/or representatives of special interest groups. Board defenders support lay trusteeship as the essence of the American way of life and propose instead that inequities be cured by improving the democratic process to give all citizens a more equal opportunity to aspire to board membership.

---

[1]J.P. Bogue, *The Community College,* New York: McGraw-Hill, 1950, p. 276.

[2]J.K. Galbraith quoted in *Focus,* May 1967, p. 23.

[3]A.C. Sherriffs, *op. cit.,* p. 11.

[4]B.L. Johnson (Ed.), *The Junior College Board of Trustees,* Occasional Report No. 16, UCLA Junior College Leadership Program, Los Angeles, Calif.: Regents of the University of Calif., Feb. 1971, pp. 36-37.

[5]"The Final Carnegie Commission Report," *Chronicle of Higher Education,* Oct. 9, 1973, p. 14.

[6]C.R. Coate, *A Churchill Reader,* Boston, Mass.: Houghton-Mifflin Co., 1954, pp. 120-121.

[7]M.A. Rauh, *op. cit.,* pp. 57-65.

[8]R. Bendiner, *The Politics of Schools,* New York: Harper & Row, 1969, pp. 11-13.

[9]R.T. Hartnett, *The New College Trustee: Some Predictions for the 1970's,* Princeton, N.J.: Educational Testing Service, 1970, p. 70.

[10]N. Gross, *Who Runs Our Schools?,* New York: John Wiley & Sons, 1958, pp. 77-78.

[11]A. Rosenthal, *op. cit.,* p. 138.

[12]K. Goldhammer, *op. cit.,* pp. 96-97.

[13]*Ibid.,* pp. 95-97.

[14]M.A. Rauh, *op. cit.,* p. 173.

[15]*Ibid.,* p. 68.

[16]R.T. Hartnett, *op. cit.,* pp. 9-18.

[17]A. Rosenthal, *op. cit.,* p. 137.

[18]K. Goldhammer, *op. cit.,* pp. 95-97.

[19]L.H. Zeigler and M.K. Jennings, *op. cit.,* p. 27.

[20]R. Bendiner, *op cit.,* p. 114.

[21]J.G. Fowlkes, "What Does the Public Expect from the Board?" *American School Board Journal,* March 1967: 8-10, p. 8.

[22]R. Bendiner, *op. cit.,* p. 108.

[23]M.A. Rauh, *op. cit.,* p. 67.

[24]B.L. Johnson, *op. cit.,* pp. 32-33.

[25]N. Gross, *op. cit.,* p. 93.

[26]Quoted in *New York Times Book Review,* New York: New York Times Company, September 16, 1973, Vol. LXXVIII, No. 37, p. 33.

[27]L.H. Ziegler and M.K. Jennings, *op. cit.,* p. 26.

[28]M. Tendler and R. Wilson, *Community College Trustees: Responsibilities and Opportunities,* Washington, D.C.: American Association of Junior Colleges, 1970, p. 4.

[29]M.A. Rauh, *op. cit.,* p. 102.

[30]M. Keaton, *Shared Authority on Campus,* Washington, D.C.: American Association for Higher Education, 1971, p. 32.

[31]*The Official Associated Press Almanac: 1973,* New York: Almanac Publishing Company, Inc., 1973, p. 276.

[32]Harold Howe II, quoted in *Education U.S.A. Special Report: School Boards in an Era of Conflict,* Washington, D.C.: National School Public Relations Association, 1967, pp. 20-21.

[33]A.B. Sykes, Jr., "Junior College Boards of Trustees, " *Junior College Research Review,* Vol. 10, No. 4, p. 1.

[34]L.H. Ziegler and M.K. Jennings, *op. cit.,* p. 26.

[35]R. Reeves, "Teachers, Politics, and Power," *Learning,* Nov. 1973, Vol. 2, No. 3, pp. 10-14.

[36]M.L. Zoglin, "Elect the Board from the Community," *Junior College Journal,* April 1972, Vol 42:7, pp. 21-23.

# CHAPTER 7
# The Board of Trustees
# and
# The Professional Staff

"Of all the agencies devised by Americans for the guiding of their public affairs, few are as vague in function as the school board . . . . For the school board is really neither legislative nor administrative in function, and only in the most limited way, judicial. Almost entirely outside these normal categories, it has homier and less precise functions, not usually to be found in civics textbooks at all: it is local philosopher, it is watchdog, and it is whipping boy."[1]

Another observer describes the situation even more forcefully: "The role of school board members is perhaps the most ill-defined in local government. The individual board member has no legal power, though the board itself is considered a corporation. The board's rights and responsibilities are rarely spelled out by the state except in the most general terms, and the board rarely undertakes to define them itself. The board's entire role and that of its individual members is simply an accretion of customs, attitudes, and legal precedents without much specificity . . . ."[2]

Although many community college people might dispute this analysis, they would be hard put to come up with a universally agreed-upon definition of the board's role. And understandably so: boards at different colleges at different times and in different places do play very different roles in the governance of their institutions. The reasons are many: the United States is a big

country, with room for lots of local variation; the community
college is a new institution, without binding traditions as to the
"right" way of doing things; and the relationship of the lay
board to the professional staff is in the process of undergoing
redefinition throughout the educational system. The board's
functions — like its powers — are in a state of flux. Indeed, it is
primarily because of their unique adaptability that boards of
trustees have survived so long as the preferred method of
governing institutions of education. This very flexibility, however, makes it difficult to generalize about the functions actually
performed by community college trustees today.

## OFFICIAL DUTIES

The doctrine of the separation of powers clearly does not
apply to boards of trustees. Some of their duties can best be characterized as legislative, a few are executive, some are clearly judicial, and others appear to be a hybrid. The area in which boards
can maneuver, it is true, has gradually been narrowed by the
encroachment of state and federal legislatures, of regulatory a-
gencies, and of the courts. But the local board's powers were
never supreme, they were always only on loan from the state —
which both giveth and taketh away. Trustees still are responsible
for taking all the steps necessary to assure the smooth operation
of their community college — unless a governmental unit with
superior jurisdiction has already preempted the field. The local
board fills in the gaps, so to speak: it legislates where others have
not done so, it sees that the directives of other governmental
units as well as its own are carried out, and it hears appeals from
those dissatisfied with any aspect of college operation.

### Goal-Setting

The foremost duty of a board of trustees — and often the least
well performed — is to establish goals for the college under its
jurisdiction. This job is poorly done because it is immensely difficult: the number of books, articles, speeches, conferences,
seminars, and workshops devoted to this topic in recent years
attests to its complexity. Due to the size and heterogeneity of the
populace served by most community colleges, the needs of its
citizens are at best diverse and at worst conflicting. Some see the

college as an opportunity for personal growth, others think of it as preparation for earning a living, and still others expect it to take the leadership in correcting social inequities. The board has the Herculean task of ascertaining the relative importance that its own community assigns to each possible goal. However, since every other action the board takes should logically derive from them, top priority must be given to the articulation of college goals.

### Future Planning

A closely related board function is to plan ahead. At first glance it seems obvious that those responsible for an institution would automatically think in terms of its future needs. But it is much easier to react to situations as they come up than to do the hard mental labor required to crystal-ball the future.

Long-range planning, admittedly, is particularly difficult for community college trustees, because they have only partial control over the destiny of their institutions. The future of a community college is more often mapped by state than by local officials. Program requirements are imposed by statewide coordinating boards, new financing arrangements are adopted by the legislature, and a changed approach to helping the disadvantaged is instituted by newly elected state officials. With so many variables beyond their control, it is hard for local trustees to see very far down the road.

Community colleges also must be ultra-sensitive to the shifting needs of their constituents. But few of us are clairvoyant enough to foresee all the changes which can occur within a ten-year, or even a five-year, period. Projected enrollments fall short when immigration fails to come up to expectations, when interest rates preclude building in an anticipated boom area, or when a lack of jobs cuts down on the popularity of one section of the country. Manpower needs are often impossible to predict: the teacher shortage of today turns into over-abundance tomorrow; engineers are a dime-a-dozen one year and eagerly sought after the next; and the local employment scene fluctuates wildly depending on the health of a single industry or the welfare of one large company.

And if this were not enough to test the mettle of those who dare to plan, the demographic makeup of the community can change, the goals of its students can change, the whole philosophy of community college education can change. All these almost seem to make long-term planning an exercise in futility. One course of action is for the board to throw up its hands in despair; the other is to recognize that the difficulties involved make it essential to devote substantial resources to the research and planning process. The resulting master plan, however, must be geared to the necessity of staying loose, of changing to meet situations not contemplated when it was developed. Trustees must plan — but with the realization that their plans are made to be altered or even discarded when changing circumstances dictate.

### Finance

Having decided where the college is going, the board must then find the wherewithal to get it there. Although the major decisions affecting community college finance are often made at the state level, local boards usually have some leeway in determining the exact amount of money available in a given year. Theirs is the task of deciding how much tuition or fees will be charged, how much of the permitted tax rate will be levied, and whether to ask the voters for permission to raise taxes. In each instance, the local board acts only within the parameters established by state laws and regulations.

The board allocates the available funds via the annual budget. By directing the flow of monies into the desired activities, the board breathes life into its adopted policies. Ideally, trustee participation in budget-making begins many months before the required completion date. The board reviews the overall goals of the college and determines what aspects of the program should be continued, expanded, strengthened, or cut back in order to better meet these goals. Staff is intimately involved in this process throughout, feeding information and recommendations to the trustees. On the basis of input from all concerned groups, the board then establishes spending priorities for the upcoming year.

Simple as this sounds, few community colleges actually develop their budgets in this way. The procedure used by most colleges is totally inadequate to cope with the complexities of a large enterprise. Some small comfort may be derived from the fact that this inadequacy is typical of other governmental agencies as well. The United States Congress, for example, recently passed a budget reform measure by a near-unanimous vote. As one news report put it, "Politicians of such differing plumage would never have agreed to change the system if it was not inexcusably bad – and it is . . . (the new legislation would) for the first time in modern history make Congress an active partner with the White House in drawing up the federal budget, instead of merely approving or denying presidential proposals or developing isolated and improvised programs on its own."[3] If you substitute "Board of Trustees" for "Congress" and "college staff" for "White House," you will have an all-too-accurate picture of the community college budgetary process.

Trustees often see the budget for the first time when it is in almost final form, too late to have any real impact on it. They receive too much information or too little, a mighty tome which obscures the total picture by listing minutiae or a few summary sheets with categories so broad as to mask the true nature of the activities funded therein. Seldom are expenditures examined in the light of college goals. Trustees usually content themselves with comparing the proposed budget with the previous year's – which may have had little to recommend it except that it was based on the budget of the year before that – and so on *ad infinitum*. Slightly less than half the community college trustees in Rauh's study felt that they had a decision-making role in formulating the budget. Another 17 percent felt that they reviewed proposals made by others or approved decisions that could not be substantially changed at that time. And five percent reported no budgetary involvement at all.[4] Clearly, boards of trustees – like the Congress – are not utilizing to its fullest this most valuable tool.

### Shelter

Another duty of trustees is to provide housing for the college program. They must decide between renting and building and among the various possible sources of money for construction – bonding, pay-as-you-go, state and federal subventions, and grants from private groups. Final decisions (assuming state standards are met) as to size, location, style, and quality of construction usually fall to the board.

## Staff

The board is responsible for determining the kind of staff a given community college will have. It establishes guidelines for choosing administrators, teachers, and classified employees. Decisions about working conditions — salary, hours, fringe benefits, sabbatical leaves, and the like — are also made by the trustees.

Perhaps the only truly executive function remaining firmly in the hands of the board is the hiring of the president of the college. Although almost all trustees feel that they alone should make this choice, many use screening committees composed of representatives from all segments of the college community to help in the selection process. There is less agreement as to the role trustees should play in hiring other members of the staff. Although they set the criteria for employment and formally ratify contracts, they seldom actually pick the people to fill the available slots. Twenty-one per cent of the trustees queried by Rauh, however, felt that they played a decision-making role in faculty appointments, while another 74 percent reported that they were in some way involved in this process.[5]

Trustees also have a role to play in the evaluation of staff. While this is accepted practice as far as the president is concerned, it is not always welcome when applied to teaching faculty. But laymen can recognize good and bad teaching and acceptable and unacceptable administrative practice — even though they may know little about the particular subject matter involved. Classroom visitations by trustees — except at the invitation of the instructor — are frowned upon by the profession but approved by the electorate. Without ever setting foot on the campus, however, trustees often hear about classroom problems via the grapevine. Their job is to feed these community reactions into the evaluation process, since this type of information may not be generated from within the institution.

## Educational Program

The heart of the board's responsibility — and the reason for all the foregoing activities — is to provide educational offerings appropriate to the needs of the community. What vocational courses will best prepare people for today's working world? What new programs should be added, which phased out? What special courses are needed by the economically disadvantaged, the different racial and ethnic groups in the area? Is enough attention paid to counseling? Are general education courses available for the non-transfer, non-vocational student? Is remedial help available for those who need it? Trustees must sit in judgment on topics such as these if they are to participate in formulating the educational program of the college.

Regulations concerning admission to the college, probation, disqualification, graduation requirements, grading practices, and academic standards fall into this category. While some states have quite prescriptive regulations in these areas, others give a great deal of leeway to the local trustees.

The board also adopts policies relating to the instructional process itself. Included here are the selection of books and other instructional materials, partisanship in the classroom, academic freedom, fairness to students – all the things that affect the way teaching actually takes place.

### Administrative Structure

The board determines the administrative structure of the college. Is it to be organized as a single unit or as a series of semi-autonomous cluster colleges? Will the traditional administrative model – president, deans, assistant deans, etc. – prevail, or is there a better table of organization? How independent will each college in a multi-campus system be? Ideally, this administrative organization is not cast in concrete the day the college opens but instead is subject to continuing review and revision by the board.

### Student Affairs and Services

The establishment of student organizations, the powers granted to student government, invitations to outside speakers, the regulation of campus publications, and a myriad of other topics relating to extra-curricular activities are the subject of board policies. On residential campuses their responsibility also includes the construction and operation of dormitories.

### Evaluation

Having provided all the ingredients to make the college operational, the board must at some stage evaluate its handiwork.

Trustees of one-room elementary schools could do this simply by questioning students at the end of each year to see if they were up to snuff in the three R's. The task of today's community college trustee is not nearly so easy. Assuming that the board has accurately assessed the goals of its community, it must then ascertain if the college program is in fact producing the desired outcome. The difficulty comes in trying to translate overall goals into a checklist against which the multiple activities of the community college can be judged. With luck, current attempts to break down each goal into performance objectives will one day provide trustees with the kind of yardstick they need to measure the success of their institutions.

While awaiting the millenium, however, trustees are usually forced to evaluate in a rather haphazard manner. It was once fashionable to assume that their responsibility was over once they had adopted the necessary policies. They were then to retire from the scene while the staff carried on. Any attempt to find out how their policies were being implemented was regarded as snooping. The accepted practice was to keep trustees out of school affairs as much as possible. They were considered hopeless amateurs and relegated to the position of establishing vague objectives which the professionals were free to pursue pretty much as they wished. Boardsmanship manuals cautioned new trustees to never, never interfere with the implementation of policy; their jurisdiction came to an abrupt end where the staff's began, with the application of their general policies to the day-to-day operation of the schools. The fallacy in this theory is that the staff doesn't always carry on — at least not in the way the board expects. The intent of a policy can easily be distorted,as every good bureaucrat knows. Sometimes this is inadvertent, resulting from a genuine misreading of the policy; sometimes it is intentional, stemming from the feeling that the board has made a mistake and the staff must try to rectify it; and at other times it is the fault of a too-rigid organizational structure which is inhospitable to certain ideas and ways of operating. On the other hand, some trustees are over-zealous in checking on policy implementation, prowling around the campus à la Sherlock Holmes in search of evidence. The line between monitoring and meddling is a fine one indeed.

Trustees are often accused of being uneven in their evaluation of college activities. They probe deeply into matters that catch their fancy while ignoring other, more important, ones. More time is spent scrutinizing the output of a copying machine than of a computer, more concern arouses by a single word in the college newspaper than by a lengthy report of the progress of students in the remedial reading program. The value of a particular field trip is analyzed within an inch of its life, while the merits of a new interdisciplinary course get short shrift. The success of a building is judged more by its facade than by the utility of its interior for learning activities. In short, trustees are seen as evaluating the college program on the basis of the trivial, the physical, the external. Some of this apparent superficiality is the result of trustees' natural inclination to stick with the familiar: their workaday experience has prepared them to understand copying machines better than computers, field trips better than interdisciplinary courses, and roof lines better than educational specifications. This tendency is ofttimes aided and abetted by staff activities specifically designed to keep trustees bogged down in the non-essential. They are, thus, kept too busy to bother with the important matters that the staff considers to be its bailiwick.

Trustees' egos also can get in the way of effective evaluation. Even when they do find soft spots in the college operation, they are often reluctant to voice their criticisms openly. They fear that such criticism will redound to their detriment, that the public will hold them personally responsible for the problem. For similar reasons the board hesitates to take issue with a president it has hired, since his incompetency might call into question their judgment in choosing him. It is obviously much safer for all concerned to ignore problems than to expose them to the probing eyes of the community.

Public pressures, however, are all in the direction of requiring more adequate evaluation. It is demanding that ways be found to hold all educational institutions accountable to the sustaining society. The lack of a perfect evaluation instrument does not relieve trustees of the obligation to meet this demand. There are available, for example, some widely accepted measures of quality against which a community college can be tested. Some of these assess input: size of the library, student-counselor ratio, adequacy of physical facilities, and quality of faculty preparation, to name

but a few. Their advantage is that they can be described in concrete terms and compared with those of model institutions or
state and national norms. In terms of output, there are follow-up
studies of students, community surveys, and accreditation reports
to help complete the picture. By utilizing all of these techniques
to their fullest, boards can go a long way towards meeting the
public's desire for educational accountability.

### Judicial Duties

Boards of trustees frequently serve as appellate bodies to hear
complaints and grievances. In the words of one author, "At the
very edge of the area of basic responsibility lurks an unpleasant
trustee duty . . . to deal with situations which have gone beyond
the capacity of the administrative machinery to handle."[6] To
trustees for final disposition come disputes between staff members
(unfair personnel practices, dismissals), between staff and students
(grades, disciplinary action), and between staff and community
(use of facilities, rowdy audiences at sports events). In some cases
the board is asked to see that its declared policy is being faithfully implemented, in others to rule in areas not fully covered
by written policies, and in still others to decide between disputed
versions of the same incident.

There is some feeling that the judicial function is, in fact, the
only one remaining to the governing board. One well-known
authority finds that boards are so hemmed in by the expanding
state and national jurisdictions, so limited by socioeconomic
factors beyond their control, and so bound by a body of generally accepted educational practice that their role has become
merely one of deciding which rule or law to apply in a given
situation. Instead of actually making policy as they formerly did,
trustees now simply apply universally accepted policy to local
circumstances.[7] And one recently suggested model for the governance of community colleges would strip the board of all its legislative and executive functions and eliminate any direct connection between it and the rest of the college governance structure.
This board would function solely as a body to which appeals
could be brought by various segments of the college community.[8]
Thus, the judicial function at least seems likely to remain with the
board of trustees for some time to come.

## UNOFFICIAL FUNCTIONS

### College-Community Relations

Trustees also perform many duties which are not outlined in the legislation governing the operation of community colleges. Foremost among these is their role as bridge between town and gown. Those same "philosophers" who enjoy debating whether community colleges are truly secondary or higher education also love to argue over whether the trustee's *primary* responsibility lies with the college or with the community. Speaking of the state university, one author says, "A basic ambivalence in the role of the trustee has not been resolved to this day. Is the trustee responsible to the university or to groups outside the university? . . . Does a trustee . . . represent the interests of the public to the university, or does he basically defend the interests of the university against the public opinion of the moment?"[9] The community college public, however, has little doubt about the trustee's major duty: it is to represent their interests, to let the college know what the community expects of it. At the same time, both those within and without the college recognize the board's duty to sustain, protect, and defend the institution entrusted to it. Actually, experienced trustees are uniquely able to do both: with one foot in the community and the other on the campus, they are in the best possible position to see the needs of both. Their ability to speak the language of college *and* community enables them to serve as interpreters whenever communications are in danger of becoming snarled. To be most effective, trustees must walk a veritable tightrope between town and gown: if they lean too far to one side, they are perceived as advocates for it alone, thus forfeiting the trust of the other. All in all, their role as the human link between school and society is one of the most subtle and critical of the functions assigned to community college trustees.

### Ceremonial Function

A closely related set of board duties can best be classified as ceremonial in nature. Cutting a ribbon to open the new highway leading into the campus, attending college events ranging from baseball to ballet, participating in a fund-raising evening sponsored

by the local YMCA — all these are board responsibilities that
cannot be carried out by surrogates. On such occasions, it matters
little what trustees say or do; the important thing is their presence. Each of these appearances is an opportunity to forge still
another link between college and community, to create good will
and mutual understanding between the two. Since descriptions
of these events are often carried by the news media, the impact
of trustee participation can extend far beyond the circle of
those present.

## Ombudsman

In addition to serving as an official court of appeal, board members frequently perform this function informally. Their position
is similar to that of the ombudsman, the official whose job it is
to investigate citizens' complaints against the government or its
functionaries. Educators, like other public employees, are sometimes guilty of forgetting that they are there to serve. Picturing
themselves as conscientious, dedicated dispensers of knowledge,
they fail to realize how formidable they can appear to the average
citizen. Students are extermely wary of alienating teachers,
who are the sole arbiters of success in their courses. They fear that
any criticism may bring retribution in the form of failing grades
or other discriminatory treatment. Thus, students often hesitate to
voice their concerns directly to instructors or administrators.
Non-teaching staff sometimes share with other governmental
employees a penchant for saying "no" whenever possible, for
doing everything "by the book," for forgetting that they are
dealing with live people with real problems. The citizen's only
recourse is to approach a board member with a request for help.
Trustees are sometimes caught between their desire to defend the
actions of staff and their equally strong wish to serve their constituency. Investigation often reveals that the two are not incom-
patible after all, that the good offices of the trustee-ombudsman
are sufficient to solve the problem. Some institutions of higher
education now employ an official ombudsman; in most community colleges, however, this duty still falls to the trustees.

## Institutional Climate

The board is also entrusted with the rather nebulous task of creating the conditions which enable the staff to perform at top capacity. In order to reach the goals of the college, human inter-action must take place. This can occur in an atmosphere of harmony conducive to fruitful activity or in one of conflict which militates against it. The morale of faculty and staff within a college is to some extent determined by the board: trustee actions can cause friction within the college or make it a pleasant place to work. One institution, for example, with salary and classroom conditions comparable to those in other nearby schools, has long been considered an undesirable location because of the actions of one trustee. He considers teachers to be lazy, good-for-nothing parasites and passes up no chance to tell them so — preferably at a public meeting. The whole tone of this institution is adversely affected by the actions of one board member. By the same token, other trustees recognize the importance of creating a climate of trust within the college and bend over backwards to do so.

### Leadership

Community college trustees, like other elected officials, are sometimes uncertain whether their duty is to lead or to follow the voters. Is it their function to ascertain the community's wishes and then to follow them blindly? Or is their responsibility the greater one of leading the citizenry on to new heights? Once elected, trustees learn many things about the educational process that the average citizen does not know. As board members grow in understanding, they may come to feel that their particular com-munity's outlook is short-sighted, that its perception of its own needs is erroneous. Does the trustee vote his conscience or his mandate, if the two conflict? One possible answer is that trustees are elected not only because of their ideological positions but because of their reputed good judgment. The electorate will tolerate a certain amount of divergence from pre-election promises and community expectations — but only so much. If trustees choose to travel far out beyond the pale, they must take steps to carry their constituency along with them. Otherwise, they may find that they are leading the community only down the road to a special election, aimed at replacing them with a more palatable representative.

**The Power Behind the Throne**

This list of trustee reponsibilities makes board membership sound onerous indeed. But the truth of the matter is that trustees depend heavily — too heavily, some say — on the college staff to perform many of their functions for them. Indeed, it is thought in some quarters that boards perform practically no functions that can honestly be described as legislative, executive, *or* judicial! At least one author believes that they have become mere legitimating agencies, explaining and justifying the activities of the schools to the public rather than vice versa. This is, in fact, often the path of least resistance for trustees. Many factors contribute to making the "hands-off" position an attractive one: trustees' lack of confidence in their own abilities in the educational arena, their need to rely on staff for all information, conscious manipulation by the administration, demands for decision-making autonomy from the faculty, pressures for conformity from within the institution, the community's general ignorance of educational matters, and the lack of a continuing constituency to monitor their voting records. When all these influences converge, a board may well become little more than a "front" serving to make the activities of the professional staff legal in the eyes of the community.[10]

Although this is an extreme view, it does serve to point up the controversy surrounding the delegation of power.*
*In the context of academic governance, "power" refers to the ability of individuals or groups to control the policy-making processes. "Authority" refers to that power which is invested in a specific office or role, while "influence" connates the use of informal rather than formal procedures, persuasion   rather than orders.[11]

Note that we are now talking about the power to *make* — not just to *implement* — policy. In the early days, of course, trustees did everything but teach the students — of necessity, since there was no one else to take care of the ancillary duties. But they gradually came to depend more and more on professional aides to run the schools for them. As noted earlier, one of the reasons for this was the desire of reformers to ensure that schools would be free from petty political wheeling and dealing. The way to do this seemed to be to appoint "professional" school managers, people who were trained experts in the operation of schools.[12] In so doing, they unwittingly laid the foundation for the conflict that exists today between two dearly-held values: "On the one hand, Americans talk much about democratic controls on education, and the school's closeness to community opinion is much stressed in the literature of educational administration. On the other hand, 'We want the best for our children' is an also-stressed popular value, one which requires surrender to the expertise of professional educators . . . this tension . . . between popular control and professional autonomy . . . in most cases results in the latter triumphing."[13] Looked at another way, the *rank* authority of the board of trustees runs smack into the *technical* authority of the professional staff — and usually is decisively rebuffed.[14]

By the mid-twentieth century the chief administrative officer of many public school systems had become the leader rather than the servant of the board. His expertise, professional reputation, and community position combined to give him an almost irresistible voice in school affairs. His rise to power strongly affected the role of the board of trustees: "The emergence of a powerful leader in the person of the superintendent . . . brought with it a concomitant decline in the position of the school board. There is a reciprocal relation between administration and board which tends to ensure that as one grows in stature the other will diminish."[15] A parallel phenomenon was occurring in higher education, with governing boards beginning to lose power to their presidents in the years immediately following the Civil War. The era of presidential dominance continued until World War I, at which time faculties began to assert their influence.

Beardsley Ruml shocked his brothers in Academe by sharply criticizing this practice in his now-famous *Memo to a College Trustee*. He noted that the major locus of decision-making in the modern university was in the departments of the faculty. However, since faculty members are hired as specialists in and advocates for a particular field of study, he questioned their competence to make decisions related to the overall, general character of the institution.[16] Moreover, he felt that their innate conservatism and status requirements militated against their acceptance of change of any kind.[17] Many observers believe that there are "even more pervasive reasons to question strong faculty control of the two-year college. If one accepts the thesis that the two-year college is a unique institution devoted to the changing needs of society, he must face the fact that faculties tend to be conservative and resistant to innovations." [18]

## Policy-Making: Theory and Practice

Current practice with regard to policy-making in the community college has been well documented by Rauh in his study of trusteeship. Participants were asked to describe their involvement in areas such as faculty appointments, budget analysis, building construction, educational programs, and instructional methods. Three answers were possible:  1) they made decisions, 2) they reviewed, advised, approved, or confirmed the recommendations of others, and   3) they had no involvement. Only in terms of long-range planning, hiring the president, and choosing architects did a majority of trustees feel that they had actual decision-making authority. In other matters most trustees felt that they were involved as described in category 2: they participated in the decision but did not make it alone. [19]

Rauh then asked them how much power they thought they should have in these areas. Only in appointing the president did trustees think they should have *exclusive*  authority, and even then some  17  percent  disagreed. [20]  Their responses changed dramatically when they were asked if boards should have *major* rather than exclusive authority over matters such as course and program changes, appointment of deans, tuition, tenure, admissions standards, professorial conduct, and student protests. A large majority wanted to have major authority over all of these except for course changes – and 43 percent wanted to include it as well. [21]

It appears that community college trustees today do not in fact exercise sole authority over the colleges they govern – nor do they want to. What they do want, however, is to have a major voice in making decisions affecting all aspects of college operation. They are apparently content with the system of "shared authority" by which most institutions of higher education in America today are governed. And this approach works very well most of the time. But what happens when those "sharing" the authority cannot agree on a course of action? If trustees and the college curriculum committee disagree over the need for new vocational programs, whose opinion prevails? If trustees and the president disagree over the need to hire additional administrators, which side wins? If trustees and the faculty senate disagree over criteria for admission to the college, who makes the decision? And if trustees and staff disagree over the need to pour more resources into counseling, who decides what will be done?

The alternatives, however, are seldom so clearly posed. They are confronted in a much more ambiguous form which leaves board, staff, and public alike unsure as to who is deciding what. The board's critical action comes when it defines the issue as either "external" — that is, related to community values and goals, implicating large numbers of people, and requiring the adoption of a new policy — or "internal" — that is, involving routine administrative procedures and falling under an existing, though possibly more general, policy. The way in which trustees perceive the issue — rather than its actual content — is critical in determining their desire for involvement.[22] If, for example, trustees see the establishment of special courses to encourage older women to return to college as a question of major community importance that is not covered by their previous policies, they will delve with gusto into the pros and cons of such a program. But if they see it as merely an extension of their basic philosophy of "providing educational opportunity for all citizens," as a question of how best to arrange the subject matter to meet this goal, they may feel that it's up to the staff to decide what, if any, special programs are needed. In actual practice, ". . . nearly all issues come to be viewed as technical problems internal to the educational system, and the market becomes biased in favor of the professional resources . . ."[23]

How does it happen that trustees are so unclear about their proper role? Even barring a conspiracy on the part of professionals to keep the board "barefoot and pregnant," trustees themselves are very much at sea as to what decisions they should be — or even *are* — making. Rauh declares that "When . . . state legislatures established governing boards as the agency of both trust and management, they created a situation that has given rise to acute symptoms of schizophrenia."[24] Small wonder that boards are confused as to their mission when their agendas alternate nuts and bolts with philosophy without skipping a beat. Item #1, for example, may have to do with setting the number of hours the bookstore will be open and Item #2 with an outreach program to take educational offerings to a hitherto unserved segment of the population. A good example of the trivia attributed to governing boards is found on this sign in a University of California parking lot: "Open only to cars with C and D stickers — by order of the Board of Regents."[25]

Some of this confusion is due to the existence of two different kinds of governing boards: *working* boards and *policy* boards. "The working board is characterized by its intention to be closely associated with most major institutional decisions. Its model lies in the corporate board of directors which is composed largely of management personnel and major stockholders. The policy board, on the other hand, delegates the decision-making process to the full-time management. The board's major role, then, lies in evaluating, criticizing, and supporting management. It may review, approve, and counsel , but it seldom undertakes the detailed consideration of data that precedes and characterizes the true decision. The confusion of purpose arises when these contrary styles are intermixed without consistent plan. Then the board is tempted into play-acting. It appears to reach decisions when in fact it is only giving *pro forma* assent to a decision made elsewhere . . ."[26]

Boards, as mentioned earlier, are often guilty of unevenness in their evaluation of college operations, so, too, with the exercise of their policy-making powers. Legally, trustees have the right to make policy covering all aspects of the college program. And, as the name "trustee" implies, they cannot give away to anyone else the powers vested in them by the people. But the gap between this theory and actual practice is wide. For the many reasons already enumerated, much of the board's policy-making authority has passed to the professional staff. In four-year colleges and universities, this authority has come to rest with the faculty rather than with the administration. In the public school system, the contrary has usually been the case. Here, however, the growing strength of faculty organizations is forcing a change. ". . . Whereas they were once relatively voiceless vassals, teachers' oral spokesmen frequently are as powerful now as a district's

professional administrators. A big city board could not conceivably enact and implement a new policy without the consent
of teacher spokesmen. In effect, teachers have been accorded veto
power over school board policy making . . . Their ascendancy was
aided by the very reforms that in an earlier era had been designed
to limit citizen participation and to improve the schools."[27] On
the surface, the situation so far as the community college board
is concerned remains the same: the professional staff is still a
major contender for power, even though the baton may have
passed from administration to faculty within the staff. There is
one difference, however, which may have important long-run
implications: while administrators can be fired for decisions
deemed wrong by the board, tenure-protected faculty members
usually cannot be.

### Policy-Making and Conflict

Partly as a result of their unclear legal mandate, partly as a
result of internal confusion, and partly as a result of pressure
brought to bear by staff (and, increasingly, by students and
community representatives), a board's actions often appear
highly erratic. On one issue, it will be a docile rubber-stamp,
on another, an aggressive decision-maker. Nowhere is the decision-
making role of each college component spelled out; it is the
result of tradition, of personalities, of "feel," of everything
except conscious planning. Since no one knows who is going to
choose to wield what power when, the opportunities for conflict
are legion.

Take the situation in which a board of trustees decides to
resume the authority that it has previously delegated to staff.
Just as trustees are unhappy when the state legislature begins to
exercise prerogatives that have long lain dormant, so are staff
members upset when boards seek to reassume functions formerly
delegated to them. Even in law, it is an accepted principle that
when someone has long used a piece of property, openly and with
full knowledge of the legal owner, he may under certain circumstances lay claim to it. Small wonder, then, that staff members
want to hold on to the authority they have become accustomed to
considering their own.

But the fact of the matter is that the board has only lent the staff the authority to perform certain functions as long as they do so in an acceptable manner. It can call in the loan at any time. When a board decides to do so, however, the result usually is "conflict and claims that the board is 'usurping power.' The claim is incorrect; what the board has been guilty of is inconsistent application of the power only it possesses . . . what is generally lacking is a description of the ebb and flow of delegation between the delegator . . . and the various delegatees."[28]

The consultation process is an excellent example of the need for making sure that all the players understand the rules of the game. No board, no matter how active or independent, can consider policy matters without extensive consultation with staff. The critical question is whether or not trustees can modify — or even reject completely — the advice of staff. Are they free to reverse a staff recommendation if, in their opinion, it is not in the best interests of the college and community? Rejecting advice is always fraught with danger, whether it comes from friends, citizens' committees, or faculty members. "Consultation, to be effective, requires delicate management and political skill on the part of all participants: the consulted party must feel that its opinions count even where they cannot be fully respected by the party initiating the consultation."[29] This becomes even trickier when the group proffering advice has come to expect that its "recommendations" will be automatically enacted into policy. In order for the consultation process to proceed amicably and effectively, all participants must know ahead of time just how much weight will be given to their advice.

Conflict between trustees and staff over their respective prerogatives is most likely to arise in the area of the curriculum. Trustees are generally conceded to have the right to participate in decisions concerning finance and construction, but their right to help plan the educational program is not universally accepted. A recent study of 23 representative institutions of higher education found that 50 percent of trustee decisions were in finance and management and only 15 percent in educational policy.[30] Rauh calls this "probably the most confused area of trustee operation . . . on one hand trustees feel the limitation of their 'lay' status while, on the other, they sense that the educational program is the essence of their responsibility and everything else is in the service of that function . . . They find themselves in the position of having legal responsibility for overseeing the program without the means for doing it."[31]

What are some of the obstacles encountered by a board that does try and make its voice heard in planning the educational program? It is here that trustees' total dependence on the staff becomes most evident. It is difficult for trustees, whose contact with the college is sporadic at best, to keep up with everything that's going on. They must rely on the board meeting to keep them apprised of important developments. But since the agenda is prepared by the staff, they decide what topics trustees will discuss. Subjects they think unsuitable for trustees' eyes may never appear on the docket. Or, if action on potentially embarrassing items is essential, they manage to come up at the end of the meeting when trustees are exhausted and the public and press have gone home to bed. It is interesting to note in this connection that, while faculty members often think of the president as the handmaiden of the board, trustees often perceive him as in cahoots with the faculty. From the trustees' vantage point, the entire staff appears to be a monolith which prefers to run its business with as little outside (trustee) interference as possible.

Assuming that trustees are able to get themselves included in on discussions of curricular matters, they must still rely on the faculty for relevant data. This is particularly true at the community college level: although everyone considers himself an expert on third-grade reading, few laymen pretend to be specialists on astronomy or nursing. Thus, trustees entering the instructional thicket run the risk of being made to look the fool: "The layman who 'takes on' the professional frequently assumes a calculated risk of being rebuffed decisively — if not put to rout — by the expert who has ready access to the pertinent data or background material."[32]

On the other hand, many observers agree that "the intelligent and open-minded lay trustee is fully capable of grasping the merits of a properly presented educational issue. Indeed, if he does not understand the proposal, it is possible that the professional proponents may not be entirely clear themselves."[33] Not only is it a dereliction of duty for trustees to avoid educational issues, but it can be a sheer waste of talent as well. One author states

that "the interest and capacity of the ablest trustees . . . are in-
effectively utilized if they are limited to the exercise of judgment on administrative and financial matters."[34] The general
opinion seems to be that trustees can and should involve themselves with the community college's educational program. Their
ability to do a really good job in this area, however, is to a great
extent dependent upon the support and encouragement they
receive from staff.

## Conclusion

Boards of trustees initially exercised almost complete authority
over the schools: they made the rules and they administered them.
Gradually, however, many of their responsibilities were taken
away by other levels and agencies of government and still more
were delegated to professional administrators and teachers. After
reaching their nadir in the mid-twentieth century, trustees began
to reassert themselves. Primarily in response to community pressures, they began to reassume some of the authority once delegated to staff. Although community college boards will never
perform the multitude of functions required of the trustees of
long ago, they can expect to become more and more involved in
the operation of the colleges as the twentieth century draws
to a close.

---

[1]R. Bendiner, *op. cit.*, p. 3.

[2]James Koerner, *Who Controls American Education?* Boston: Beacon
Press, 1968, p. 122.

[3]"Bold Reforms for Better Budgeting," *Time,* vol. 103, No. 13, (April
1, 1974), p. 17.

[4]M.A. Rauh, *op. cit.*, p. 70.

[5]*Ibid,* p. 70.

[6]*Ibid.,* p. 8.

[7]H.T. James, *op. cit.*, pp. 6-7.

[8]S. Nichols, "Model for Participatory Governance for Community
Colleges"U.C.L.A., 1971, p. 4.

[9]H.L. Hodgkinson and L.R. Meeth, *op. cit.*, p. 9.

[10]A. Rosenthal, *op. cit.*, p. 171.

[11]R.T. Hartnett, "Trustee Power in America" in J.L. Hodgkinson and L.R. Meeth, *op. cit.*, p. 27.

[12]James W. Guthrie, "Public Control of the Schools: Can We Get it Back?" *Public Affairs Report,* Bulletin of the Institute of Governmental Studies, University of California, Berkeley, Vol. 15, No. 3, June 1974, p. 2.

[13]F.Wirt and M. Kirst, *The Political Web of American Schools,* Boston: Little, Brown & Co., 1972, p. 95.

[14]L.H. Zeigler and M. K. Jennings, *Governing American Schools,* North Scituate, Mass.: Duxbury Press, 1974, p. 148.

[15]R. Bendiner, *op. cit.*, pp. 85-6.

[16]Beardsley Ruml, *Memo to a College Trustee,* New York: McGraw-Hill, 1959, pp. 6-7.

[17]*Ibid.,* p. 61.

[18]C. Blocker et al, *op. cit.,* pp. 189-90.

[19]M.A. Rauh, *op. cit.,* p. 70.

[20]*Ibid.,* p. 62.

[21]*Ibid.,* p. 63.

[22]L.H. Zeigler and M. K. Jennings, *op. cit.,* pp. 156-7.

[23]*Ibid.,* p. 157.

[24]M. Rauh, "Internal Organization of the Board," in James A. Perkins., Ed., *The University as an Organization,* New York City; McGraw-Hill, 1973, p. 229.

[25]*Ibid.,* p. 229.

[26]*Ibid.,* p. 229-30.

[27]J.W. Guthrie, *op. cit., p.* 3.

[28]J.E. Corbally, Jr., "Boards of Trustees in the Governance of Higher Education," *Theory and Practice,* Vol. 9: 239-43, pp. 241-242.

[29]H.L. Mason, *College and University Government,* New Orleans: Tulane University, 1972, p. 13.

[30]L. Heilbron, *The College and University Trustee,* San Francisco: Jossey-Bass, 1973, p. 22.

[31]M.A. Rauh, *The Trusteeship of Colleges and Universities,* p. 24.

[32]A. Rosenthal, *op. cit.,* p. 430.

[33]M.A. Rauh, *op. cit.,* p. 35.

[34]John J. Corson, *Governance of Colleges and Universities,* New York: McGraw-Hill, 1960, p. 106.

# CHAPTER 8
# Hamilton County:
# A Multi-College District
# in Action

In 1946 the young men on the faculty of Central High School came back from service in World War II. Several of them had spent their wartime years in California. By chance, all had lived in communities which offered the first two years of college in connection with the high school program. Their special interest in education led them to study these programs and eventually to entertain the hope that Central High School might one day emulate them. All were overjoyed to find on their return that others too had visited the Promised Land and come back with the same dream.

They made some converts among the non-veterans on the faculty and, emboldened by this success, approached the superintendent with their idea. To their surprise, he was enthusiastic at the thought of being the first to transplant this marvelous idea to the east coast. The Board of Education seconded the idea *con brio,* lured at least partly by the thought of the tuition dollars they would pick up from the multitudes of GI Bill holders abroad in the land. Whatever their motives, the "powers-that-be" moved promptly into action and the first college classes were offered in the fall of 1947.

Central City College, as the fledgling institution was named, at first offered its wares in whatever nook or cranny remained after the regular high school courses were housed. By 1949, however, it had outgrown these accommodations and was ready for quarters of its own. The most appropriate building seemed to be the old vocational high school, and the decision was made to turn it over to the growing college. As part of the deal, it was completely renovated and furnished with the most up-to-date equipment. Thus, Central City College came to have a strong vocational orientation and gained fame throughout the area for the excellence of its occupational programs. Its faculty was also aware that some students planned to go on to four-year institutions and still others, with less certain goals, wanted mainly a general education. As a result, CCC always offered a balanced program to its student body.

During the fifties the central city followed the national pattern of declining in population while its suburbs grew rapidly. By 1962 the city itself had dropped from 450,000 to 430,000, while the rest of Hamilton County soared to a record 550,000. Two years earlier the state legislature, realizing that its higher education system was lagging behind the rest of the country, had passed a Junior College Bill. It encouraged agencies of local government to join together to establish colleges and made funds available for this purpose. The eight school districts in Hamilton County approached the Central School District with an offer to jointly sponsor a college program in the area. Their suggestion was accepted with alacrity, since CCC too was anxious to tap the new state funds.

The new Hamilton County Junior College District was formed in 1962 and its 15 trustees — one-third appointed by the governor, one-third by the city council, and one-third by county commissioners — took office. Their first step was to acquire sites for the new campuses they expected the district would need. The combination of state and local funds provided for construction was more than generous, and the opening of Eastside College in 1967 was quickly followed by that of Southwest College in 1969.

During this period vocational programs in the health sciences were very much in vogue. Colleges offering them were secure in the knowledge that they were contributing to the welfare of society at large as well as of the individual student. Since each of the colleges in the Hamilton District wanted a share of the action, the health-related programs were parceled out among them. The long-established course for medical secretaries at City College was expanded to a medical assistants' program and radiologic technology was added. When Eastside opened, it housed the new nursing programs, for RN's and LVN's. And Southwest was proud to be the first junior college in the state to offer preparation for dental hygienists as well as dental assistants.

This happy equilibrium was not to last for long, however. In 1970 the Members' Medical Plan, a pre-paid health care program, announced plans to expand from its base in the midwest to several major eastern metropolitan centers. One of these was to be Hamilton County, and an option was taken on a site for a 600-bed hospital just one mile from the Eastside campus.

The faculty in the Life Sciences Division — of which the nursing program was a part — was greatly excited by this news. The tremendous job potential of the new hospital was obvious. With the consent of the college president, the Advisory Committee on Nursing was expanded to include all of the health careers field. Its membership was increased by adding doctors active in the county medical association, workers in various health agencies, and representatives of the Members' Medical Plan, who had already set up a local headquarters.

From the beginning the rejuvenated committee — renamed the Advisory Committee on Health Careers — was inclined to Think Big. This was the chance of a lifetime to design an ideal paraprofessional program and they were not going to let it slip by. For once, time was in their favor: they had several years headstart on the opening of the hospital, scheduled for the fall of 1976.

The Advisory Committee spent almost two years developing and refining a proposed master plan for a comprehensive health careers program at Eastside,   making it by far the best researched project in district history. Faculty members worked closely with all governmental, educational, and volunteer agencies affected by the hospital's establishment. Thus, even at this early stage their plan was assured of broad community support.

The final proposal had several parts. The medical assistants' program would be moved from City College and expanded to include preparation for workers in the fields of medical transcription and medical records. The radiologic technology program would also be transferred to Eastside, where it would be joined by programs in inhalation therapy, nephrology, physical therapy, and nuclear medicine. As entry programs to these highly technical areas, Eastside would offer courses for emergency department aides, operating room technicians, nurses' aides, and nurses' assistants. The existing RN and LVN programs would be doubled in size. The most innovative part of the package had to do with the newly-emerging specialty of physicians' aides: Eastside would start off by offering training for pediatricians' and orthopedists' assistants.

Their timetable was tied to that of the hospital. In order to have paraprofessional personnel available for its opening, the first class would have to graduate no later than June of 1976. This meant that students in the AA degree programs would have to start by the fall of 1974, those in the one-year programs by 1975. Eighteen months start-up time — for seeking grants, acquiring equipment, remodeling facilities, and planning the curriculum — was considered minimal. Thus, all plans would need final approval by January of 1973. As of January 1972 this goal seemed readily attainable and they congratulated themselves on having more than enough time for even the most unexpected of circumstances.

By March of 1972 the Advisory Committee felt that its brainchild was ready for a public debut. Basically, the plan was to make Eastside the center for all of the Hamilton District's vocational offerings in the health field. This consolidation, in their eyes, would have many advantages. It would permit the offering of core courses which would be economical for the college and educationally sound for students. The latter would be able to explore the many possible kinds of health careers before choosing among them. In addition to this horizontal flexibility, opportunities for vertical mobility would be assured by the development of career ladders. Thus, any student in Hamilton County with an interest in the health field could come to Eastside to find his or her appropriate niche.

This plan had already been approved by Eastside's Life Sciences Division; the next step was to present it to the college Curriculum Committee. There it met with a most enthusiastic reception, above and beyond their already high expectations. An impartial observer, however, would not have found this surprising: Eastside's Curriculum Committee had long since become a "You scratch me,

I'll scratch you" body. Its members asked penetrating questions and even occasionally sent proposals back to the author for modification, but they never turned anything down. As long as some case could be made for inclusion in the curriculum, they deferred to the wishes of the sponsoring division. Since all proposals had to go through several more layers of decision-making before being adopted, the campus Curriculum Committee did not feel responsible for determining if college resources were being most efficiently used. Nor were they always in a position to do so, since the complexities of their multi-campus district made it difficult to see how actions in any one college fit into the overall picture. Thus, the health careers program passed its first test with flying colors, partly due to its merits, partly due to the peculiarities of the college's governance system.

The rejoicing, however, stopped at the borders of the Eastside campus. Rumors soon began to fly at City and at Southwest to the effect that Eastside was trying to "take over" in the health field. The next scheduled meeting of the District Curriculum Committee – the next hurdle for the proposed health careers program – was six weeks hence. This group met at regular intervals to evaluate the district-wide effects of curricular changes proposed by the individual colleges. Even under the best of circumstances this process generated a great deal of hostility; it was incredibly time-consuming and none of the colleges liked having its sibling institutions and/or the central office tell it what courses to offer. The old-timers on the faculty particularly resented this intrusion into campus affairs. When the Hamilton District was conceived, all concerned – trustees, faculty, and administrators alike – made a commitment to respect the independence of the several campuses. Despite the size of the new district, they would make sure that it did not succumb to the disease of bureaucracy. The central office staff would be kept small and controls on the colleges minimal. Over the years, however, the exigencies of the situation demanded some backing off from this policy. The desire for economy led to the establishment of multiple coordinating mechanisms – committees, councils, and boards – to avoid duplication of services. The desire for excellence led to the creation of various district-level positions designed to provide help to all the colleges: directors of instruction, of research, and of vocational education and their backup staffs were added to the original skimpy table of organization. All these groups and individuals, of course, would want to have a finger in the pie that was a-baking at Eastside.

Thus, it was with some trepidation that the Eastsiders approached their first away-from-home test. They were aware of the concern their proposal was causing at City and Southwest but assumed it would blow over when its many benefits were properly explained. The District Curriculum Committee was composed of the dean of instruction and two members of the Curriculum Committee from each college plus the district directors of instruction, research, and vocational education. Eastside's presentation was made by Mark Hardesty, chairman of the Life Sciences Division, backed up by several instructors. It was lengthy and a full hour of questions followed. The representatives from City and Southwest felt that, as usual on a matter of such importance, they should consult with their home Curriculum Committees before reaching a decision. Since the DCC had other matters to consider, it was decided to forego discussion of the health careers program until the next meeting. Since it was now the end of April and the college Curriculum Committees would not meet again until mid-May, the DCC would not reconvene until fall. The Eastside members suggested a special session devoted exclusively to the health careers proposal, but were turned down — end-of-the-year calendars were too busy to accommodate an extra meeting of anything short of the National Security Council. Disappointed but hardly surprised — delay was becoming a way of life in the Hamilton District, some felt - they resigned themselves to putting their project on the back burner for the summer.

Although its sponsors felt as if nothing were happening, the pot was in fact continuing to boil. The City College Curriculum Committee met in early May, Southwest's in mid-month. Committee members had many questions, most of which exhibited their skepticism about the new program. How valid were the manpower statistics supplied by governmental agencies? Was not oversupply of medical paraprofessionals appearing in other parts of that country? What if Members' Medical Plan's expectations as to membership were not fulfilled? Aren't vocational programs in the health area notoriously expensive on a per student basis? Wouldn't it inconvenience many students to have all these programs concentrated in one part of the college district? Mr. Hardesty and his troups were invited to be present at these meetings and felt they had satisfactory replies to all questions. Committee members, however, were apparently not convinced. They wanted to check back with the divisions they represented before committing themselves to a pro or con position. This, of course, would be impossible to do before the end of the term, thus precluding further action until fall.

At this point the health careers program seemed to be making progress backward. In April it had reached the District Curriculum Committee; in May it was headed back to the classroom level on each campus. Its sponsors, however, like the rest of the academic community, were too occupied with end-of-term activities to be greatly upset. Since they, too,were scattering for the summer, they were not too unhappy to have their project go into temporary hibernation.

Classes resumed in early September. With the first month serving as the annual shakedown cruise, committee meetings were not scheduled until October. The health careers group arrived at City's Curriculum Committee meeting early, confidently expecting to be first on the agenda. To their amazement, they found that they were not on the agenda at all. Their amazement turned to suspicion when they found the situation repeated the following day at Southwest. However, they soon learned that this was not a dastardly plot to scuttle the health careers program; the machinery had simply broken down. When last seen, the proposal was moving toward the division chairman's office. Just who was responsible for retrieving it from this exile was anybody's guess. This, too, was not unprecedented: other good ideas had started the trek from the classroom to the board room in good condition, gotten lost in the maze of requirements en route, and were never heard from again. Too many people, however, had too much invested in the health careers program to let this happen. They traced their proposal to the in-basket of the dean of instruction at City and to the top drawer of the chairman of Southwest's Curriculum Committee. This detective work having consumed some ten days, the items concerned could not be heard before the November meetings of the college Curriculum Committees.

This time, finally, the health careers program was the main item on the agenda. The arguments of the previous spring were rehashed but with greater emphasis on the negative. Although the discussion presumably centered around the educational value of the program, there was also a hidden agenda: committee members were really worried about its impact on their own colleges. City, of course, violently opposed the loss of its medical assistant and radiologic technology programs to Eastside, since both its faculty and its students would be hurt by such a move. Southwest cast a negative vote for more subtle reasons: it feared that someday its dental programs, too, might be spirited away and it didn't want to establish a precedent for such piracy. In addition, there was an underlying concern that the money budgeted for constructing a Performing Arts Center at Southwest might be diverted to special health careers classrooms at Eastside. This is not to say that Curriculum Committee members were not sincerely interested in the welfare of students. But they were convinced that their own colleges were doing a good job of meeting student needs; it was their duty to reject anything that might jeopardize their ability to continue doing so. In light of this, it was not surprising that both Southwest and City turned thumbs down on the health careers programs as a whole. They complimented its authors for their initiative and encouraged them to implement those phases which did not infringe on the activities of the other campuses.

This action was, of course, immediately reported back to Eastside. After much conferring, all agreed that it was time for the president of the college, Dr. Robert Alfredo, to step in. Up until this time he had seen his role as supporting and encouraging his staff; as long as things were going well, his time and talents could be deployed elsewhere. Now, however, his active involvement was clearly called for.

His first action was at the weekly meeting of the three college presidents and the district chancellor, Dr. Omar Peterson. The latter used his presidents as if they were staff officers, and every Tuesday was spent in helping him resolve district-level problems. In addition, Thursday mornings were devoted to District Cabinet meetings, where top college and central office administrators were joined by students, faculty, and non-academic employee representatives. Added to these were a host of special meetings called to respond to specific situations such as salary negotiations, personnel problems, or community protests. The presidents found that some weeks they barely set foot on their own campuses.

At the presidents' meeting Dr. Alfredo described his staff's unhappiness over the treatment its pioneering health careers proposal was getting on the other campuses. Its prospects now looked dim, since it was unlikely that the District Curriculum Committee would override the opposition of both City and Southwest. The makeup of the Committee made this almost a certainty, since its opponents held six of its twelve seats. The unwritten rule was that consensus — grudging, oftentimes, but consensus still — was necessary for action to be taken. Unbeknownst to most members, there was a by-law somewhere that officially required seven favorable votes to get a proposal out of the Committee.

But that was still far in the future. Dr. Alfredo's job for now was to try and arouse some enthusiasm for the health careers program among those higher up in the district hierarchy than even the District Curriculum Committee. Expecting its decision to go against him, Alfredo was preparing his next line of defense. The presidents had a long but inconclusive discussion of the matter. Both Dr. Tim Shepo of Southwest and Dr. Martin Cohen of City voiced objections similar to those of their campus Curriculum Committees. Dr. Peterson, as was his wont, was non-committal. He had a strong aversion to making unpopular decisions, and this promised to be one of the least appealing in a long time. He fervently hoped that something — anything — would happen to get him off the hook. Perhaps the three presidents would each give a little, perhaps someone would come up with a dream solution that would delight all concerned, perhaps some *deus ex machina* would take it completely out of his hands. In any case, it was too soon to start worrying. He exhorted the presidents to give it their closest attention and to work toward a compromise.

Meanwhile, Hamilton's committee machinery ground slowly on. Dormant over the summer, the District Curriculum Committee moved smoothly into gear in October. The participants took their seats at the table and picked up the discussions of the previous spring as if they had occurred but yesterday. The colleges' positions were as predicted: Eastside solidly in favor, City equally strongly opposed, and Southwest mainly opposed. The chink in the latter's armor was one faculty delegate who really liked Eastside's proposal. Since she was not bound by the vote of her Curriculum Committee, she could pursue an independent course. The directors of instruction and vocational education threw their weight behind it: this type of consolidation was exactly what they had been urging for some time. The director of research, however, did not share their view. He was miffed because the whole proposal had been developed without consulting his office. If this were to become standard practice, there would be no need to have a district-level director of research. This was, in reality, just one of many skirmishes in the continuing battle between the campuses and the central office over research: the former preferred to have the money allocated to the colleges to do with as they saw fit, while the latter advocated the centralization of all research.

Many hours of discussion served only to intensify the areas of disagreement. Although it had never been necessary in the previous three years of the DCC's life, the decision was finally made to take a vote. City College cast three "no" votes; Southwest recorded two "no's" and one "yes"; Eastside cast all its votes in favor; and the directors split, with instruction and vocational education in favor and research opposed. Dr. Shepo was widely known as a stickler for the rules and, true to form, he had looked up the by-laws and informed his delegation of the legalities of the situation. Lacking seven affirmative votes, the proposal would die. The chairmanship – which alternated each meeting – was held by one of the City College representatives, who accepted Shepo's interpretation and adjourned the session.

Observers from outside the academic world might have assumed that the comprehensive health careers program was now dead. This, however, was far from the case. It was at such times of stress that both the strengths and weaknesses of the district's governance system became apparent. If the District Curriculum Committee had the authority to make binding decisions on all curricular matters, this would indeed have been the end of the road for the health careers concept. But no one on the staff of the colleges or of the district had that authority; it was legally

the prerogative of the Board of Trustees. As the elected representatives of the people of Hamilton County, they could not
permanently delegate any of the powers entrusted to them by
the public. Like all lay boards, they did delegate to any and all
staff members, up to and through the chancellor, the power
to *recommend* action. But every action taken by groups or
individuals in the name of the college was theoretically revoca-
ble by the Board of Trustees. The advantage of this system was
that the desires of the public — as interpreted by the trustees —
would always take precedence over those of the staff. Internal
politics, in the final analysis, would have to give way to the
democratic process. The disadvantage was that this system was
imperfectly understood and unevenly implemented. No one
knew when the Hamilton trustees would choose to exercise
their legal prerogatives. The members of both college and district
Curriculum Committees had given their time and effort in good
faith to study the health careers program. Since neither the
Board nor the chancellor had overriden any of their decisions
in recent memory, everyone assumed that they did not have the
right to do so.

The chancellor and the college presidents, however, understood
the situation very well. When word of the DCC's turndown
reached the Advisory Committee's community members, they
were outraged. They, too, understood but vaguely the internal
decision-making process: their assumption was that Eastside
College was the master of its destiny and that it could therefore
plan programs as it saw fit. Their immediate reaction was to
suggest contacting the trustees, but Dr. Alfredo assured them
that there were still other avenues to be explored. His next step
would be to put it on the agenda of the District Cabinet meeting.
Since it was now getting into December, the faculty sponsors
were becoming increasingly nervous about the time element,
but no one could think of a way to hurry up the process.

The District Cabinet was the final clearinghouse for recommendations being readied for board action. Members represented
all segments of the college community. They were chosen by
their peers but spoke as individuals at Cabinet meetings. No
official votes were taken, since the purpose of the Cabinet was to
give advice to the chancellor, who was free to follow or dis-
regard it as he saw fit.

This time the Cabinet had plenty of advice for him — all conflicting. It ranged from "Scrap the health careers program today" to "Start it tomorrow." Between these extremes were sandwiched some valid concerns and some constructive suggestions. The district personnel director was worried about the human dislocation that would be caused by switching some programs from City to Eastside. Although district policy clearly stated that personnel could be transferred among colleges to meet changing needs, the shifting of schedules and of people always brought discord in its wake. The director of business services was worried about the calendar: if new construction or even remodeling was required, his office would be responsible for getting it done on time. The Advisory Committee had supposedly taken this into account in its timetable, but he knew from experience that construction always took twice as long as even the most pessimistic could predict.

As usual with a large group — there were 19 present — it was impossible to package these ideas into a compromise proposal on the spot. Although some wanted to consign it to oblivion right then and there, others thought it deserved further study. Finally, the Cabinet threw up its collective hands and agreed to pass the whole matter on to a later session. The promoters of the project were enjoined to come back with a new proposal that would speak to the concerns expressed by the various Cabinet members.

For the next few weeks — interrupted only by the Christmas recess — Dr. Alfredo's office was the scene of almost round-the-clock meetings. Faculty members on the Advisory Committee plus those community representatives who could get away from their regular jobs plus the district director of vocational education searched for ways to cut the health careers program without emasculating it. Their goal was to placate the other two colleges; continued opposition from both would surely mean defeat for the whole program. They concluded that enrollment projections might possibly justify the existence of two courses in medical assisting, one at City College as at present, and one at Eastside to fill the increased demand generated by the new hospital. In return for the radiological technology program, which was essential to Eastside's plans, City College could have the veterinarians' assistant course slated in the district master plan for implementation at Eastside in 1975. Finding a way to mollify Southwest was not so easy, since their fear was that *any* funds diverted to construction elsewhere would scuttle their own building plans. Thus,they would have to oppose any expansion at Eastside until their own needs were met. In light of this, the Advisory Committee decided to concentrate on getting City College in their corner and, effectively, to forget about trying to curry favor with Southwest.

Throughout this period the Tuesday presidents' meetings were becoming increasingly bitter. Dr. Shepo became more and more shrill in his denunciation of the health careers program. Dr. Alfredo kept the chancellor and his fellow presidents informed of the Advisory Committee's progress. Sr. Cohen expressed his satisfaction with the proposed changes and promised his personal backing. But he wanted to run it through his President's Council at City first, before making a public commitment. This, of course, meant further delay, but City College's approval was much more important in the long run than a few lost weeks.

Dr. Shepo remained adamant, despite considerable prodding from Peterson. The latter hated to have to enter a dispute among the colleges — indeed, he preferred that such disagreements never got to the point where he even heard about them. It was essential that as chancellor he be perceived as guardian of the welfare of all the district's students, not as an advocate for one college or another. This image of impartiality, which he had carefully cultivated, could easily be destroyed if word got around the Southwest area that he was responsible for postponing their Performing Arts Center. Finally, goaded more by Dr. Shepo's intransigence than by the merits of the case, Peterson gave his tentative blessing to the proposal, contingent on agreement by City College. It would, of course, still have to run the gamut of the District Cabinet and the Board of Trustees. The former's approval was almost assured, assuming that City was in Eastside's camp, and the latter usually rubberstamped the chancellor's recommendations.

These negotiations spilled over from December into January and it was not until February that all was in readiness for the Cabinet. The meeting was convened in an atmosphere of tense expectation. The rumor — exaggerated but difficult to refute —

of the impending demise of the Performing Arts Center had spread quickly across the Southwest campus. Administrators, faculty, and students in the Fine Arts Division had used the holiday period to lobby their friends on the Cabinet. Alfredo feared that his newly-forged coalition with City College might dissolve under the pressure; there was still some disaffection there, particularly among those staff members most intimately affected by the proposed changes.

It became apparent early in the meeting, however, that everyone except Shepo and his cohorts was getting pretty tired of health careers and wanted to get on to other matters. Labor negotiations have long known that fatigue forces more solutions than does logic. In less tense situations, boredom — a closely related phenomenon — often serves the same purpose. It was clear to all that Eastside's health careers program was not going to fade away; the Cabinet's alternatives were to approve it or to continue wrangling over it. The majority of the delegates opted for the former. They gave polite but cursory attention to Shepo's presentation and moved quickly to the revised proposal itself. Even the director of research, who didn't like to be on the losing side if he could help it, this time gave his stamp of approval. Although no vote was taken, it was apparent that all but the Southwest contingent considered the matter closed. Their advice to the chancellor was unambiguous: get on with it as quickly as possible.

There remained but one hurdle: the Board of Trustees. Their next meeting was in early March. This meant that the program was already several months behind schedule. If, for any reason, the Board failed to give its O.K. at that meeting, the health careers program would be in real trouble. Although Hamilton's trustees professed their dislike of approving important proposals the first time they came before the Board, Peterson knew that he could convince — "brainwash," some might call it — them of the urgency of this project. Really, the only time they gave their chancellor a hard time was when he failed to inform them in advance about a controversial issue. Usually accused of excessive docility, even they tended to bridle when confronted with the unexpected — especially if any unpleasantness was involved. Thus, any time he could find to fill the Board in on the background of the health careers controversy would be time well spent. He would send the members a report — not too short, but not so long as to risk going unread — on the program immediately. Between now and the Board meeting he would find some pretext for calling each trustee on the telephone; he would steer the conversation so as to be able to appraise their individual reactions to the program.

The only possible fly in the ointment was public pressure from residents of the Southwest area. Peterson took pains to make his feelings on this topic known and, at the next presidents' meeting, left Shepo with the distinct impression that the blame for any such outcry would be laid at his door. He was to reassure his colleagues and his constituency that the Performing Arts Center would at worst be postponed, not cancelled, and that further opposition would be not only futile but counterproductive. Peterson, for his part, would undertake to prepare the Board for the possibility of protest at the meeting should Shepo fail to quell the potential opposition. Taking no chances, Alfredo would make sure that the community members on the Advisory Committee were there to counteract, if necessary, the impact of citizens from the Southwest area.

And, for once, these well-laid plans did not go awry. Shepo had gotten the message and cooperated fully. One drama teacher from Southwest did take it upon himself to plead for early construction of their new facility, but he had been admonished by Shepo to be brief and positive in his comments. In the absence of opposition from the public, the presence of the Advisory Committee was noted and its members thanked for their services — by now far above and beyond the call of duty. Mr. Johnstone, the trustee who lived nearest to Southwest College, was somewhat nervous about possible adverse reactions from his neighbors. Another trustee suggested that they might show their continuing affection for Southwest by adopting a motion reiterating their intention to build a Performing Arts Center there àt the earliest possible opportunity. All were delighted with this felicitous suggestion and the motion passed unanimously. Confident that this gesture would placate even the most skeptical of Southwest boosters, the trustees then, with consciences crystal-clear, voted to approve the establishment of a comprehensive health careers program at Eastside College.

# CHAPTER 9
# Internal Politics

All institutions of higher education have at least one thing in common: a complex internal decision-making process that is poorly understood by participants and observers alike. As Beardsley Ruml put it, "when depicted on an organizational chart, a college resembles any other institution following the hierarchical pattern . . . (it) resembles the bureaucracy of government, military, religious, and business organizations. On close examination, however, the reality is found to be quite different. The 'chain of command' in a college is at most a tenuous line of influence."[1] Sociologist Victor Baldridge describes its power structure as "a hodgepodge of interacting, overlapping, and often conflicting influences."[2] Other terms found in the literature on academic governance are "inchoate," "shifting," "ambiguous," "murky," "poorly-defined," and, perhaps most apt of all, "organized anarchy."

## Multiplicity of Authority Structures
This confused state of affairs is due in part to the existence of a dual — perhaps soon to become a triple — authority structure in higher education. Community colleges do exhibit many of the characteristics of the bureaucratic or hierarchical model typical of other organizations; but their governance process is also heavily influenced by the faculty and, increasingly, by the student body.

The administration of the community college is endowed with the authority delegated to it by the people of the state through the legislature and the institutional governing board. Like other bureaucratic networks, the structure is multi-layered, with a formal chain of command running from the trustees through the president, the deans, and the department chairmen right down to individual faculty members. Each official claims and exercises authority over a given area.[3] This structure is pyramidal in nature, concentrating authority and decision-making in the hands of those few operating near its top. The administrative domain usually extends to the interpretation of external influences, the definition of priorities, the allocation of resources, the issuance of directives governing faculty and student performance, and control of the resultant process through the measurement of results.[4] Unlike other managers, however, school administrators usually do not have the right to dismiss staff members working under their jurisdiction.

But this is only part of the picture. Side by side with this hierarchical structure stands one based on professional expertise and manned by teaching faculty. The right to participate in decision-making is here conferred not by the political community but by the community of scholars. Eligibility is earned by becoming a member of the teaching faculty, which, in turn, is dependent upon attending the appropriate graduate schools, acquiring the requisite degrees, and receiving sufficiently laudatory recommendations from professors. Entree may also sometimes be gained through successful vocational experience or eminence in a particular field.

Those matters most commonly under the jurisdiction of faculty are admission standards, curricular structures, course content, examinations,degree requirements, faculty selection, retention, and promotion, work schedules, and the evaluation of performance. The independence of this professional authority structure is enhanced by the principles of academic freedom and tenure.[5]

### Relative Strength of Hierarchical and Professional Networks

At the elementary and secondary school levels the hierarchical model is dominant. The dual structure is typical of four-year colleges and universities, with the professional network often having broad powers. Community colleges are arranged along a continuum stretching between these two models. Not surprisingly, considering their administrative heritage, they tend to be concentrated near the high school end of the spectrum. Richardson states that "A careful examination of two-year colleges reveals

an absence of these parallel structures for decision-making accompanied by pervasive administrative dominance."[6] A recent
study in New York State confirms this statement: researchers
surveyed eight public two-year colleges and found that influence was highly centralized at the top levels of administration.
By contrast, the four-year colleges included in the study were
characterized by a control structure in which professors viewed
themselves as exerting almost as much influence as top-level
administrators.[7]

Although this was typical of most community colleges as recently as a few years ago, the situation is changing fast. Many
people involved in the junior college enterprise considered it to be
"higher education" from the very beginning, even though it was
not officially so designated until  much later. As a result, the
desire to emulate the governance structure of the university has always been present. The dream of collegiality, of decision-making
by the community of scholars, is a powerful and enduring one.
Thus even the most "backward" of today's community colleges
exhibit some elements of the dual authority structure common in
American higher education.

Academic Senates, almost unheard of in the junior colleges of a
decade ago, are now commonplace. Collective bargaining laws and
agreements are based on the assumption that teachers play a role
in educational decision-making. Committee systems similar to
those in the university are in widespread use. The growing strength
of state and national faculty organizations enables their members
to insist on meaningful involvement in the institutional governance process.

In some community colleges the pendulum has swung far in this
direction, placing faculty firmly in the driver's seat in matters of
instruction. Woe betide the dean who unilaterally tries to shake up
the remedial reading program! If he wants to effect change, he has
to find a real live teacher to act as sponsor and then convene a
committee to deliberate on the idea. In many colleges all new
courses must be approved by the curriculum committee; it can be
as difficult for an administrative proposal to negotiate its way
through this group as for the proverbial camel to get through the
eye of a needle. And Heaven forbid that college presidents should
have ideas! Any display of intellectual vitality on their part is

considered unseemly by some, who prefer them to woo the local Kiwanis Club or prowl the halls of the state capitol. These are, if course, extreme cases, as are the colleges where the president's word is still treated as it were a Decree From On High.

### Student Structure

As if the existence of *two* parallel authority structures were not enough to thoroughly confuse the issue, there is now appearing a *third* — embryonic, but alive and growing: the student structure. Historically, this has been a separate operation, dealing with the social rather than the academic side of life, with the frills rather than the essentials. In the late '60's, however, students began to demand participation in the *real* governance of the college. As a result, while still responsible for extracurricular activities and services, students are now being integrated into the internal decision-making process as well.

College committees (curriculum, academic standards, budget) and presidential advisory groups are being reconstructed to include student representatives, academic senates invite them to membership, all-college councils composed equally of administrators, faculty, and students are being established, student spokesmen are appointed by their own elected officers rather than by the college staff, and items of college-wide importance are referred to the student council for study and recommendations. This is not an all-inclusive list of student participation in governance, but it is illustrative of the approach most community colleges are taking. Regardless of the formal structure, it is true that in many places student involvement is still token, more an opportunity to object to unacceptable policies than to help formulate desirable ones. But in others, students are welcomed as full members of the decision-making group and their ideas are solicited and adopted.

### Coordination of Authority Structures

At times these authority structures — administrative, faculty, and student — seem to function in splendid isolation. The faculty decides how many courses to offer in each field and what size class is appropriate for each subject; the administration decides the level of maintenance to be provided for the college's buildings and grounds; and student body officers decide how much of their funds go into child-care and athletic programs.

But people are now beginning to question the existence of purely "educational" or "business" or "extracurricular" sides of the college enterprise. Faculty, students, and admininistrators are all discovering that *everything* has a price tag, that money spent for gardeners can't be used to support small classes, that the subsidy students withdraw from the college newspaper must be replaced by funds from the regular budget, and that salary increases and high-cost vocational programs may be in competition for the same scarce funds. Thus, the faculty *is* interested in the amount of money spent on buildings and grounds, the administration *is* interested in how student officers allocate their funds, and students *are* interested in the level of faculty salaries.

The realization that all aspects of the college operation are interrelated has led to cooperative decision-making. In the heyday of administrative autocracy, presidents usually ruled their feifdoms with the aid of a cabinet or council composed of top-level aides. As the faculty began to seek power, they realized that access to this inner sanctum was the key to meaningful involvement. And as students followed them in this quest, they too sought entry to this council. In most institutions their requests were eventually granted and the council was expanded to include student and faculty as well as administrative representatives. Thus, what was originally a personal advisory group to the president metamorphosed into a mechanism for coordinating the advice of all segments of the college community.

An added impetus to the utilization of a central clearinghouse is the legal structure within which most community colleges operate. In order to give official standing to the decisions of the staff, the board of trustees must often ratify them at an open board meeting. When proposed changes in the grading structure, for example, are presented to the board, members often want to know what students and deans as well as teachers think of them. To avoid unpleasant surprises at board meetings, each constituent group finds it desirable to check with the other interested parties before asking for final board approval. The desirability of presenting a unified proposal to the board of trustees thus serves as a powerful incentive for the various internal segments to cooperate in policy development.

### The Critics

Although few thoroughly understand the complex system that is community college governance, many are prepared to criticize it. In this the community college is not alone; McGeorge Bundy has observed that "the distribution of authority and responsibility among the various members of the university is now in question as it has not been for generations."[8] Indeed, one can say without fear of contradiction that academic governance at all levels has few admirers in America today.

Some of the critics fault institutions of higher education for being undemocratic, feeling that the faculty should be accorded a larger role in decision-making. Others feel that, based on the university's experience, this leads to less, rather than more democracy: a student spokesman states bluntly that "there is a second step that should be taken if we are to build a more democratic university: the power of the faculty must be restrained."[9] Defenders of the status quo argue that colleges have come a long way from the almost monarchical rule that characterized them in earlier times. They claim that academic governance is already far more democratic than any other comparably complex enterprise like business firms or governmental bureaucracies.

Specifically, the administratively-dominated type of community college is accused of being unresponsive to the needs of both faculty and students.[10] Faculty-dominated institutions, on the other hand, are said to be run by small cliques that are frequently casual about their accountability to the college's constituency. Those who subscribe to this belief warn that control over academic decision-making is becoming as lopsided in one direction (faculty) as it once was in another (administration).[11]

The dual decision-making structure of many colleges is criticized for its tendency to encourage the segments to operate in isolation, causing them to lose the ability to adapt and change so as to remain relevant to today's world.[12] Still other observers charge that administrators and teachers together have begun to constitute an educational bureaucracy. They accuse them of adopting the attitudes and attributes normally associated with bureaucratic behavior, including placing the interests of the service group above those of the group served. One author writes that "the educational bureaucracy has achieved notable success in driving the public school structure toward a monolith under oligarchic control. It is to be doubted, indeed, whether the bureaucracy plays so important a role in the governance of any other public undertaking in America."[13]

## Student Role

One of the most widespread criticisms of the community colleges is that they have failed to include students in their internal governance system. This oversight is not too surprising, considering the history of the junior colleges. They were originally an appendage of the high schools, and thus their decision-making structure was copied from that of a system which served a much younger group of students. Even the university, however, which has no such historical excuse, has done little more to welcome student participation. It was not until recently that the message to "include students in" began to come through loud and clear to all institutions of higher education.

Proponents of an expanded faculty role in community college governance at least know what they're getting into. Senior institutions have a wealth of experience in this field and thus offer a variety of models for the community college to follow. But when it comes to student involvement, all are sailing in uncharted seas.

The first problem confronting a community college that sincerely wants to involve students in governance is their extreme heterogeneity. The dean or committee chairperson attempting to assess student opinion is sorely tempted to ask, "Will the *real* community college student please stand up?" Is she Dawn Davis, 18, just out of the local high school, a full-time student working towards her B.A. degree? Or Tom Viskovich, age 30, a veteran of the wars and of the world, just now finding the need for formal higher education? Or is she Elizabeth Samuels, in her late forties, holder of a bachelor's degree unused for 25 years while she raised children, taking one or two courses to give new direction to her life? Or Angie Velasquez, encouraged by a special program for women to take up where her education left off 30 years ago, in the fifth grade? Or Marshall Stevens, mid-fifties, whose job skills are fast becoming obsolete, working full-time but taking night courses in the latest technology? Or Jim and Ruth Valentino, retired couple, keeping up with the world by taking two or three short courses each year on ecology, philosophy, or travel? Or Margie Branscomb, divorced mother of three, taking courses part-time to get back into the job market and off welfare? *Will* the real community college student please stand up?

Heterogeneous as the student body may be, it is, of course, no more so than the community that sustains the college. And, as indicated earlier, it is not essential that representatives be exactly *like* those they represent. On the other hand, they must know the needs of their constituents and serve as their advocates. On the community college campus, however, students have little time to get to know each other. The candidates themselves have usually not been around long enough to establish a reputation for themselves or to know much about what makes the college tick. Thus, as compared with students at four-year colleges, the relatively short tenure of community college students poses an extra barrier to meaningful participation in governance.

Also, the elective process, imperfect at best, often becomes a travesty on the community college campus. If the turnout of voters at regular elections is deplorably small, the number voting in many student body elections is minuscule. There are sometimes special obstacles that exclude some students from the voting process altogether, such as requiring the purchase of a student body card or setting inconvenient times and places for the election.

Another problem unique to community colleges is the difficulty they have in separating out their students from the general public. Citizens of all ages alternately enroll at the college and melt back into the community. By contrast, students at four-year colleges and universities have certain characteristics that set them off from the surrounding populace: they relocate themselves from their homes to the college's locale; they are heavily concentrated in a narrow age range; their primary if not entire occupation is that of a student; they usually attend school full-time; and they spend several consecutive years studying at a single institution. Thus there is on campus a relatively stable and easily identifiable student body. Those elected to participate in government are usually upperclassmen; their peers have had ample opportunity to get to know them and to pick representatives who share their point of view. Aspirants to office have had sufficient time to get to know the workings of the college they attend.

The weakness of community college students as participants in the governance process is thus related to the fact that they are almost indistinguishable from the rest of the local citizenry. This, however, can also be their strength: as full-fledged members of the voting public, they can influence the college from the outside via the board of trustees. They have an "ace in the hole" that their counterparts at other types of colleges and universities lack: via the ballot box they can bring pressure to bear on trustees, administrators, and faculty alike.

In addition to the practical problems posed by the transiency of the student body, there is a philosophical dilemma involved in giving substantial power to a group that is "here today and gone tomorrow." Faculties change but slowly, unless the college is growing rapidly; administrative turnover, except at the very top, tends to be small; and the citizenry, except in boom or bust areas, is relatively stable. All these groups have a long-term stake in their community college and thus would not be tempted to sacrifice its future for short-term gains. This, of course, is also true of some students, who expect to be associated with the college in one way or another for many years. But many students, too unsure of their plans to know if they will pass this way again, have no such commitment. They may prefer to take actions whose benefits are immediately apparent even if it means using up the inheritance rightfully due those who will come after them. The student role in college governance must thus be designed to safeguard the interests of future as well as current generations of students.

### Politics

As noted earlier, it is difficult to define the boundaries of each segment's authority, since they are determined more often by tacit agreement than by explicit grants of power. And it is even more difficult to decide exactly how much authority the participants *should* have. But even if we were able to agree upon the domain of each group and describe it with precision, we would still not have a complete picture of the decision-making process. Everyone knows that even two colleges operated by the same unit of government, with the same formal governance structure, will do things quite differently. There is apparently something individual about each college's power structure — its "feel," its "style," — that cannot be captured on a table of organization. People sometimes refer to these elements as "the politics of the situation," and they may be nearer to the truth than they realize.

So far the decision-making system has been described as a combination of bureaucratic (hierarchical) and collegial (professional) structures plus an emerging student component. This analysis still leaves unanswered the question of how interaction takes place within and among these three networks. Baldridge suggests that it might be fruitful to look at this process from another angle, to examine it using a political framework for analysis.

### Levels of Participation

He postulates the existence of four levels of participation in college and university politics. First are the officials (also known as authorities or administrators) who are "committed by career, lifestyle, and ideology to the task of running the organization. They constitute by far the most politically active segment . . . . and have the most influence over organizational decisions."[14] At the second level, on the faculty side of the aisle, are a group he calls the "activists, a relatively small body of people intensely involved in the university's politics even though they do not hold full-time administrative posts . . . (they) serve as part-time authorities by working in the official committee structure and in the complex of advisory councils . . . (they are) usually faculty members who lead dual lives as professors and amateur organization men."[15] Other observers dub this group the "oligarchs" and portray them as a sort of ruling elite. At the third step down the activity ladder are the "spectators," the sideline watchers who are interested in the formal system to the extent of attending faculty meetings and voting but stop short of getting actively involved. And, finally, "at the lowest level of participation, are the "apathetics" — those who never serve on committees, rarely show up for faculty meetings, and in general could not care less about the politics of the university."[16]

These categories, of course, closely resemble those used earlier to describe the general public and its relationship to the schools.

As we delve into the college governance process, we come on a scene that is even more reminiscent of the community politics described in Chapter IV. There are, for example, within each community college many competing subcultures: remedial education, multicultural programs, occupational training, counseling, and the liberal arts, to name but a few. Viewed from another angle, the community college "family" is split along the lines of administration vs. faculty, younger faculty vs. older faculty, bright students vs. average students, faculty committed to intellectual endeavor and faculty committed to social action, the curriculum and the extracurriculum, and so on.[17] Often these interest groups do not come into conflict because they simply are not concerned with the same issues. They do clash, however, when they begin to compete over scarce resources or attempt to redefine their areas of influence. These various subgroups can be thought of as political parties or, even more accurately, as the *ad hoc* groupings typical of school politics, each having its own special orientation, values, and goals.

## The System in Motion

College administrators claim and exercise authority in many areas and, thus, by themselves make many critical decisions. The faculty oligarchs operate similarly: under normal conditions they are permitted by their colleagues to rule with relatively little interference. But even under the most placid of exteriors, political action is going on in the background. Administrators daily make decisions based on their formal authority — but they also protect their flanks by consulting with any group that might challenge their actions. Faculty leaders do the same: they are careful to work closely with any subgroup that might possibly take umbrage at their decisions.

But when the various subgroups come into real conflict, structure, this political action becomes overt. If the business department wants a new computer that the liberal arts faculty feels partment wants a new computer that the liberal arts faculty feels is a waste of money, if the curriculum committee refuses to approve an experimental course that younger faculty members want to teach, if administrators refuse to permit students to invite certain speakers to the campus — then the fur begins to fly.

Once a problem surfaces, partisan groups form to advance their respective causes. Each group marshals its forces for the ensuing struggle. Officials have at their command bureaucratic power of various types: control over the budget, the power to appoint officials, the ability to insulate potentially cooperative partisan groups, and persuasion, cooptation, and sanctions. Faculty and students have recourse to resolutions from various organizations, pressure on individual administrators, appeals to professional and discipline-oriented associations, and publicity to enlist the support of community groups. Even those faculty and students described as "spectators" enter the fray at this point, finally goaded to action by a stimulus strong enough to shock them out of their lethargy.

The first fight often comes over the location of the decision-making authority. Once that has been determined, the outcome may be a foregone conclusion. An academic senate, for example, dominated by the liberal arts faculty will almost certainly decide against buying the new computer, while a dean of instruction known to favor expanding the college's technical programs can be counted on to approve it.

Some of the interest groups basically trust those in positions of authority to make the correct decisions; they enter the battle only to give support. Others are neutral in their attitude towards the authorities; they are confident that by offering appropriate inducements they will get favorable decisions. Some, however, despair of the officials' ability to make or execute what they consider to be desirable decisions. This group may try to change not just a specific action but the goals of the college itself; in order to do this they may attempt to oust those officials who hold the authority to make the decisions in question. Their basic weapon is coercion, since they have abandoned hope of attaining their goals by less violent methods.

Those on the hot seat try to anticipate these pressures in order to neutralize them before they can do any harm. They sometimes gain freedom of action by playing off various groups one against the other. But they are equally likely to be caught in the crossfire of a skirmish not of their own making. A conflict that starts out between two subgroups — journalism students and the English Department, for example — may end up by pitting either or both factions against the official who is called in to referee the action.[18]

None of these activities are listed on the college's organizational chart or on the agenda of any of its committees, councils, or cabinets. But they are what really makes the institution go round. As Hartnett puts it, "in the quest of power in the academy, the basic ground rules appear to be not too different from those that apply to community power, political power, or any other kind of power; to the extent that the group can marshal substantial, relevant support for its cause, its chances of success are increased, whether it has authority or not . . . No one group really "holds" the power or even a certain portion of it. Power is situation-dependent. The allocation of the power in certain situations depends on which group can marshal the most support for its position."[19]

### People

There is still another strand that gives color and interest and variety to the rich tapestry of community college governance: the personalities of the individuals involved. The importance of individual men and women in the history of the world has long been debated. The romantic view holds that they do indeed play a critical role in determining its course. Thomas Carlyle gave perhaps the most sweeping expression to this sentiment when he wrote that, "The history of the world is but the biography of great men." Assuming this to be even partly true, the community college is a true mirror of the world outside. Each college has its own version of the Churchills who rally their comrades, the Hitlers who lead them astray, and the Gandhis and Napoleons and Solomons who inspire and organize and enlighten them.

Some of these leaders are active in the official governance system — either as faculty or administrators — of the college. Others, however, wield power way out of proportion to their formal roles. They hold no office, chair no committee — indeed, they refuse assignments when offered — but that does not diminish their influence. No major decision is made, no crisis resolved without prior consultation with them. Their authority stems from the fact that they have earned the respect of their colleagues.

At the opposite end of the spectrum are the gadflies who carp at everything that goes on, whether or not their opinions are solicited. They are often secretly desirous of attaining official positions of authority and are frustrated by the fact that none is offered. As a result, they use the squeaky wheel approach to make their influence felt. And once in a while, more or less by chance, their nattering does strike a responsive chord with their colleagues, elevating them temporarily to the leadership role they seek.

Another highly visible group within the community college are those with a mission: year in and year out they plug their vision of what the college should do, of what the world should be like. While most of what they say falls on deaf ears, they,too,eventually may find a receptive audience.

Baldridge describes some of the other types who enliven the college scene: "The artful administrator who keeps them smiling as he puts the knife in their backs, the star professor who demands his way even if it disrupts a department, the ambitious young man who prods the faculty councils, the imaginative free-thinker who generates new ideas — these and many more are the exciting personal elements that go into the political dynamics of the university."[20]

His reference to the "artful administrator" illustrates still another way in which personalities influence the governance process. As indicated in an earlier chapter, fruitful interaction among co-workers is more likely to occur if they trust each other. Although some governance systems facilitate the development of a climate of trust more than others, no structure can guarantee it. In the final analysis, this can only be done by those holding leading positions in the college: the administrators, faculty "oligarchs" and student officers. Just why and how some people strike their colleagues as trustworthy while others do not is hard to explain, but the phenomenon exists nonetheless. Sometimes rapport among co-workers, even potentially antagonistic ones, is established immediately; sometimes it never comes. These personal relationships exert a subtle but strong influence on the entire decision-making process. They also help explain why the essence of the governance system of a community college cannot be satisfactorily captured by even the most detailed description of its formal structure.

## Conclusion

The internal governance system of the community college features an administrative staff that exercises considerable authority, a faculty whose power varies widely from one institution to another, and a student body bent on becoming a much more active participant. The areas in which each group exerts its authority are nebulous and shifting, defined more by happenstance and history than by conscious decision. The three power structures are tied together at the top by some kind of all-college cabinet or council composed of representatives of each segment.

Critics of this system advocate further sharing of administrative powers with the faculty and student body. Faculty advocates feel that by virtue of their expertise they are best qualified to make educational decisions. Students claim that those for whom the college supposedly exists have practically no voice in determining its course. Some, however, are fearful of giving too much power to the faculty, warning that excessive faculty control can be at least as onerous as administrative dominance. Others point out the danger of delegating too much authority to students whose involvement with the college is necessarily short-lived. And administrators, caught in the squeeze between the expanding domains of students and faculty, are distressed by their growing inability to move the college in the directions they deem best.

But these formal aspects of the governance structure do not tell the whole story of decision-making within the community college. In order to understand the interaction that goes on within and among constituent groups, we must look at it as a political process in which *ad hoc* groups and strong individuals often have as much influence as the formal decision-makers.

*REFERENCES*

[1]Beardsley Ruml, *op. cit.*, pp. 55-56.

[2]Victor Baldridge, *Power and Conflict in the University*, New York: John Wiley & Sons, 1971, p. 50.

[3]*Ibid.*, p. 114.

[4]R. C. Richardson, Jr., Clyde E. Blocker, and Louis W. Bender, *Governance for the Two-Year College*, Englewood Cliffs, N.J.: Prentice-Hall, Inc., 1972, p. 109

[5]T. R. McConnell, "Faculty Government" in H. L. Hodgkinson and L. R. Meeth, *op. cit.*, p. 99.

[6]R. C. Richardson, Jr., Clyde E. Blocker, and Louis W. Bender, *op. cit.*, p. 102.

[7]Peter Blomerly, "The Junior College Department and Academic Governance," *Junior College Journal*, Vol. 41:6, pp. 38-40, p. 40.

[8]Quoted in H. L. Hodgkinson and L. R. Meeth, *op. cit.*, p. 99.

[9]Robert S. Powell, Jr., "Student Power and Educational Goals," in H. L. Hodgkinson and L. R. Meeth, *op. cit.*, pp. 70-71.

[10]R. C. Richardson, Jr., Clyde E. Blocker, and Louis W. Bender, *op. cit.*, pp. 183-184.

[11]Earl J. McGrath, "Who Should Have the Power," in H. L. Hodgkinson and L. R. Meeth, *op. cit.*, P. 196.

[12]R. C. Richardson, Jr., Clyde E. Blocker, and Louis W. Bender, *op. cit.*, p. 184

[13]A. Rosenthal, *op. cit.*, pp. 288-289.

[14]Victor Baldridge, *Power and Conflict in the University*, p. 177.

[15]*Ibid.*, pp. 177-178.

[16]*Ibid.*, pp. 177-178.

[17]John D. Millett, *Strengthening Community in Higher Education*, Washington, D.C:- Academy for Educational Development, 1974, p. 7.

[18]Victor Baldridge, *Power and Conflict in the University*, pp. 136-137.

[19]Rodney T. Hartnett, "Trustee Power in America," in H. L. Hodgkinson and L. R. Meeth, *op. cit.*, pp. 35-36.

[20]Victor Baldridge, *Power and Conflict in the University*, p. 162.

# CHAPTER 10
# Midwest
# Community College
# Leads the Way

Midwest Junior College was founded in 1935, part of the spurt of junior college activity that marked the Depression years. Located in the heart of the Upper Midwest, it serves the city of Three Falls and the surrounding Maxwell County. The population of Three Falls has doubled in the last forty years and now stands at 120,000, while the rest of the county has remained stable at just over 50,000. The economy is diversified, based almost equally on agriculture and small industry.

The first thirty years of Midwest's life were relatively placid. The people of the area were rather awed by the honor of having a real "college" in their midst. The state university, some 200 miles away, was not readily accessible to most of them.

The president of Midwest — a homegrown product who had worked up through the high school as math teacher and track coach — was typical of the good administrators of his day, outgoing, dedicated, autocratic, more a doer than a thinker. The board of trustees remained stable over the years: an incumbent running for re-election was never defeated. Membership reflected the makeup of the area's "Establishment," although none thought of it in those terms. The five trustees were usually successful farmers, small businessmen, professional men, and at times one housewife-civic worker. Most were Republican in politics and relatively conservative in their outlook on life. The teaching and administrative staff was a solid one, made up primarily of the best of the local high school faculty wooed away by the challenge and prestige of the junior college.

In 1968 Midwest's long-time president retired and the college entered into a new era. The outgoing president encouraged the trustees to seek outside the college and even outside the state for their new leader. A majority agreed that it was now time to join the mainstream of the burgeoning community college movement. As a result of a well-planned and thorough search, they were able to hire Dr. William Jenkins, a 40-year old vice-president for instruction in a large California college, who was a native of the Upper Midwest anxious to return home.

Dr. Jenkins moved slowly but surely to bring Midwest Community College (the name had been changed the year before as part of the "New Look") into line with the times. Benefiting from the passage of a state law encouraging the growth of community colleges, Midwest expanded rapidly. As the teacher shortage was just then beginning to turn into a glut, the college was inundated with applicants from all over the country. Jenkins, although working closely with deans and department chairmen, actually chose most of the new faculty. They were mainly young, bright, educated at some of the country's best universities, and cosmopolitan in outlook. Encouraged by generous policies on conference attendance, they kept up-to-date in both disciplinary and professional matters despite their relative geographic isolation.

One of the ideas "in the air" at this time was non-punitive grading. This somewhat imprecise term usually refers to a grading system in which students receive credit for courses they complete successfully,but do not receive a penalty grade (variously defined as D and/or F) for courses in which they do not do well. The names of courses attempted but not passed may or may not be entered into students' records, but in neither case do they affect their grade-point averages.

The first Midwest faculty member to become actively interested in bringing no-penalty grading to the college was Marvin Anderson, a composition and literature instructor. Discussions with his colleagues in the Communications Department convinced him that others on the faculty shared his views. He decided to send up a trial balloon at the next departmental meeting.The reaction, predictably, was mixed, with his previously identified friends expressing enthusiasm and others expressing various degrees of approval, skepticism, and opposition. The response was generally favorable enough so that he felt encouraged to pursue the idea.

The next appropriate step seemed to be to take the matter to the Faculty Senate. This was a relatively new group, growing out of the old Faculty Association, but it was beginning to play a major role in college affairs. The proponents of non-punitive grading — Anderson had now persuaded five cohorts to join with him in a steering committee — prepared descriptive materials and distributed them to the 20 Senate members. When the topic was broached at the next Senate meeting, the reaction — to the surprise of its advocates — was decidedly negative. In particular, the Science, Mathematics, Business, Engineering, and Health Careers Departments felt that it would be detrimental to their programs. The counseling staff, on the other hand, jumped on the bandwagon immediately and with enthusiasm. The "pro" and "con" groups were also divided — although not entirely — along the lines of age and number of years with the college.

Those opposed to the change were genuinely concerned about its effect on student learning: they feared that the elimination of failing grades would decrease motivation, fill classes with "goof-offs" who would take teaching time away from the serious students, and give Midwest a bad image in the eyes of the public on whose support it depended. Senate members did agree, however, to take it back to their constituencies for discussion and return with direction from them to the next meeting.

All this brouhaha within the faculty did not go unnoticed by the students. In fact, those teachers favoring the measure actively enlisted student help in getting it through. The "steering committee" met with the officers, explained their proposals, and requested Student Council backing. The latter responded with alacrity: this was one topic on which the opinion of their constituents was sure to be nearly unanimous. After all, what student had anything to gain from having a D or F on his or her record? To give meaning to their endorsement, the Council decided to mount a campaign to convince other groups within and without the college of the rightness of their cause. First on their list was individual action, with each Council member contacting the teachers they knew best. Then would come an appearance before the Faculty Senate, some letters to the local newspapers, and a request to the president to plead their case before the Board of Trustees.

About this time the whole business seemed to its originators to be getting out of hand. They had not counted on the extreme enthusiasm of their student backers and were especially dismayed by their attempts to bring the general public into the discussion at this stage. The approximately two-thirds of the faculty who opposed no-penalty grading were irritated by the increasing pressure put upon them by their students. The dean of instruction, who considered such matters to be in his bailiwick, was insulted because he had not even been asked for his opinion on the matter. Some of the trustees were beginning to get phone calls, and the president spent his entire lunch hour at the local service club explaining that the whole thing was still in the discussion phase.

With this much ferment going on, some official action had to take place. A major difficulty was that no one quite knew who had the authority to make a decision of this kind, and everyone wanted to get into the act: the Faculty Senate, the dean of instruction, the dean of students, the Student Council, the president, and the Board of Trustees all had some reason to feel that grading standards should fall within their jurisdiction. There was considerable disagreement over the appropriateness of involving the Board of Trustees. Since it was purely a question of academic standards, some argued, it fell entirely within the purview of the faculty. Those advocating non-punitive grading adhered most firmly to the principle of faculty control, in part because they expected the Board to oppose it. Its opponents, on the other hand, were willing to sacrifice this principle in the hopes of getting Board backing for their stand. The president knew that he *had* to take it to the trustees for final approval: they would insist on acting on anything that had aroused so much public interest. And, although the Board in general followed the advice of the professional staff on academic matters, it still had the legal right to step in whenever it saw fit.

Fortunately, there was one place where all these differences could be ironed out — or at least aired. That was the College Council, an advisory group created by President Jenkins soon after

his arrival at MCC. All the internal segments of the college community — the Student Council, represented by its president and
vice-president, the Faculty Senate, with its president and vice-
president as representatives, and all the major administrators
held voting membership on the Council. This was the customary
route for all policy matters going to the Board of Trustees for
action: the Council would come up with a consensus recommendation or, if that proved impossible, a majority and a minority
proposal.

With a date set for the showdown, backstage activity became
frenetic. The dean of instruction was among those who opposed
the change. Urged on by those faculty members who shared his
view, he sought aid in fighting it from the state and regional level.
His first step was to consult the executive director of the Board of
Higher Education, under whose aegis the community colleges operated. The director assured him that there were no state objections to non-punitive grading. Although the legislature had em-
powered the Board of Higher Education to set minimum academic
standards for community colleges, the Board chose to write these
so as to permit as much latitude as possible to the local governing
board. A telephone call to the office of the state Community College Association brought the information that two other colleges
in the state had already changed over to a similar system without
any unfavorable reaction from state officials. He next contacted
the Midwest Regional Accrediting Association to ascertain their
interest, if any, in this matter. The response was negative, in the
sense that M.R.A.A. did not require usage of any one specific
grading structure. Calls to those colleges to which most M.C.C.
graduates transferred elicited the fact that the whole question of
non-traditional grading systems was under study by their Office of
Admissions. At this point they did not expect that the new system
would adversely affect the chances of Midwest's students for
acceptance.

The dean of students, on the other hand, was a staunch supporter of non-punitive grading. He and his staff gathered information from journals and from the few other schools using it for
presentation to the College Council. Also included was a resolution from the state Student Personnel Officers' Association en-
dorsing the concept of non-punitive grading. Student and faculty

lobbying went into high gear in an effort to turn around the "no" votes among Faculty Senate members. When the Senate convened, as scheduled, the debate was long and acrimonious; the results were closer than before but still showed a small majority in favor of the *status quo.*

The College Council convened the following Wednesday at 2 p.m., its regular meeting time. Dr. Jenkins had asked representatives of each side to prepare position papers as an aid to the Council's discussion. Copies of these — unfortunately not ready in time for distribution prior to the meeting — were passed out and members looked them over as they waited for the entire group to assemble. Everyone was then given an opportunity to state their feelings and a general debate ensued. The discussion was still hot and heavy two hours later when, as usual, members began to drift away. It was decided to set a special meeting to continue the discussion, since other college matters had to be taken up at the next regular Council session. After the usual hassle over finding a date when everyone — or even a majority — was free, an evening meeting was agreed upon. Three members were given the task of attempting to draw up a proposal that would provide the desired benefits and at the same time meet the concerns of the skeptics. This formidable task was assigned to the dean of instruction, representing the "cons," the student body president, representing the "pros," and the president of the Faculty Senate, who was personally a "pro" but officially represented the faculty's "con" position.

The Council was reconvened ten days later and the results of their labors were presented. Basically, they had come up with a compromise proposal combining the no-penalty grading concept with safeguards to prevent students from repeatedly taking courses without doing enough work to get credit for them. All but the dean of instruction professed themselves willing to accept this proposal. The Faculty Senate president, however, felt obliged to return once again to his constituency for approval. At this point the students cried "Foul!" They suspected that they were getting the run-around; at the rate things were going, they predicted that they and all their friends who had worked so hard on this proposal would be long gone from MCC before it was adopted. They accused the faculty president and the dean of instruction of stalling in hopes that they could marshall enough support to defeat it. Dr. Jenkins, who heretofore had confined his role to that of a skilled moderator, indicated his whole-hearted support of the idea and promised that he personally would not let it get lost in the shuffle. The meeting ended with a decision to call still another special meeting one week hence in order to prepare the final policy to take to the Board of Trustees.

This final meeting was a model of harmony. A majority of the Faculty Senate had finally approved the new grading policy, mollified by the inclusion of provisions to prevent abuse. The dean of instruction fought a lonely rearguard action but soon realized that his cause — at least for the moment — was hopeless.

Due to the thorough preparation that had already been done, the proposed policy, along with supporting documents, was mailed to the trustees ten days prior to the Board meeting. This was, of course, not the first time they had heard of it: two members had already called Dr. Jenkins to complain that they were hearing from their friends that Midwest wasn't going to flunk anybody anymore. Their lack of information had embarrassed them, since the public expects its trustees to know all about *everything* that goes on at the college. At the Board meeting the president presented the new policy in general outline only, as much for press consumption as for the trustees, who had presumably studied it ahead of time. As was often the case, one member had not done his homework; his questions revealed his ignorance and forced Dr. Jenkins to go over facts that everyone else in the room already knew. At this point, the individual personalities and viewpoints of the five trustees became critical: three of them had to be convinced to support the new policy or all their hard work would go for nought.

The chairman of the Board was Dr. John Martindale, 50-ish, a respected physician. With a busy general practice, he did not have too much time to devote to Board matters and usually followed the lead of his fellow trustees. Thomas Jenks was a retired farmer, well-to-do, very conservative, very conscientious in his Board duties. Marian Warrenton was in her forties, educated at exclusive eastern schools, married to the scion of the leading family in Three Falls. James March, at 35 the youngest member of the Board, operated the downtown haberdashery he had inherited on his father's death a few years earlier. And Thaddeus Hopkins, in his early sixties, was a semi-retired insurance man who was a great reader and a sort of cracker-barrel philosopher.

Initial reaction to the president's recommendation was mixed. Mrs. Warrenton expressed some enthusiasm, Dr. Martindale was non-committal, and the others indicated that they had major reservations about it. Individuals and groups present (all from within the college) were invited to present their arguments and to answer questions from the Board. After some two hours of discussion, it was agreed that the Board had to get on with its other business. In any case, a major policy like this was never adopted or rejected on first hearing; the trustees would use the two-week period preceding their next meeting to think it over and test out the reactions of the public.

Newspaper headlines the next day shouted "No More F's at MCC". The story that followed was accurate and informative, but many readers retained only the impression conveyed by the heading. It aroused an unusual amount of public interest. Residents of Three Forks were normally rather diffident about expressing their opinions on community college issues, since most had not themselves had the opportunity of continuing their education past high school. However, everyone who had ever been inside a classroom could understand the meaning of "No More F's."

Both staff and trustees received many "messages" from the public over the next two weeks: in person, by phone, and by mail. The trustees, unsure themselves as to the right course of action, went out of their way to solicit the opinion of friends and acquaintances. Dr. Martindale heard from his patients, who were from all walks of life and all parts of the county, Mr. Jenks talked with cronies at the Grange and church meetings he and Mrs. Jenks attended, and with his favorite granddaughter, a student at MCC; Jim March was in contact with other members of the MCC Alumni Club (he was the only alumnus among the Board members), the downtown businessmen, and the general public who patronized his store; Thad Hopkins still travelled around the county and kept in touch with many of his insurance customers, but his understanding of people and their needs came mostly from books; Mrs. Warrenton's social contacts were with the well-to-do and socially prominent of the area, but her extensive volunteer work put her in touch with the least fortunate members of the community as well.

In addition to these casual communications, each Board member received a few phone calls advocating one stand or another. Mrs. Warrenton began to suspect an organized telephone campaign when she received seven calls from acquaintances who, she knew, belonged to one particular political organization. Dr. Martindale was contacted by the state senator representing Marshall County; a horrified constituent had called to solicit his aid, and he wanted to turn the whole problem over to the Board chairman.

Organizations outside of the college were also beginning to sit up and take notice. They were in the main opposed; they shared the concerns of the faculty and added a few of their own. One of the latter was that "I had to suffer through it, so you should too" syndrome: life would be all too easy for today's students if there were no danger of failing a course. They also feared the effect on the taxpayers' pocketbooks; their presumption was that the average student would end up taking — or at least sampling — more courses before transferring or receiving the A.A. degree. Potential employers of Midwest graduates worried that future transcripts would give a false picture of students' abilities; they felt they needed to know not only the courses in which applicants had succeeded but also in what areas and how often they had failed.

When word of the proposed grading changes first reached the public ear, several members of the University Women's Club decided that it merited investigation. Accordingly, they set up a study group, invited local speakers on both sides, imported a professor of education from the state university, and distributed pertinent articles. Their consensus was that it was a worthwhile experiment that should be tried. At their next general meeting, a resolution to that effect was directed to the MCC Board of Trustees.

The Businesswomen's Club took the opposite tack. Urged on by some of their members who taught in Midwest's Business Department, they passed a resolution condemning the change. Their action was duplicated by the County Real Estate Association, which also had close ties with the college's real estate instructors. Both groups feared the quality of the highly respected programs now offered would be diminished. They were joined in their opposition — but for different reasons — by the Taxpayers' Association. The latter considered this just one more battle in the long war to keep college costs from soaring out of sight.

When the day of reckoning arrived, the Board meeting opened to a full house. Most of those present were students and staff; the others were spokesmen for organizations that had taken a formal position on non-punitive grading and one or two citizens with strong personal feelings on the topic. This was an unusually high turnout on the part of the general public: most citizens either did not know about college issues, did not care about the outcome, or trusted the elected Board to do what was best for all concerned.

The Board chairman first called for members of the audience to make known their feelings on the proposed policy. Representatives of the various community organizations that had passed resolutions read them aloud. Students and faculty presented some new figures purporting to show greater unanimity in their ranks than had prevailed earlier. The Alumni Club urged opposition to the policy; they feared that the good reputation of MCC, on which their future ability to get jobs depended, would be lowered by this action. A dramatic highlight of the session was a plea by Martin Beidekker, a highly respected mathematics instructor at MCC, for support; he described how he had had a change of heart during the debate and now felt that the new grading system should be given a try. A spokesman for the Minority Coalition said that his group was in favor because many of their young people had difficulty during their first semester at MCC. The elimination of D's and F's would make it easier for them to adjust to college standards without ruining their grade-point averages for all time. A dissident group of evening students — not representing any organization but purporting to speak for many of their fellows — indicated opposition. Their classes were often overfull already and they did not want their professors' time to be further diluted by the addition of students on a shopping expedition. Tempers rose and at one point it looked as if two of the speakers might have a go at it outside; Dr.

Martindale, however, was able to calm the incident by making a joke of it.

Following these comments, Dr. Jenkins reiterated his recommendation of the previous week. Mrs. Warrenton moved adoption and, after a long pause, Mr. Jenks seconded "to get the matter on the floor." Discussion was heated, with Mrs. Warrenton now an ardent supporter, Mr. March in opposition, Hopkins thoughtful, and Jenks his usual taciturn self. Martindale was kept busy restraining the audience, which tried to interrupt each time a trustee made a statement they didn't like. He was clearly teetering and would probably vote with the majority, whichever way it went.

The discussion seemed to be getting nowhere until Hopkins announced that he had a compromise motion to offer. It seemed to him that the only objection people had to the new grading system was that it *might* bring about some undesirable student behavior. He suggested that they find out by instituting it for a two-year trial period and deciding on its permanence at that time. The administration would be directed to draw up criteria for evaluation and to keep the appropriate statistics over the next two years. Mrs. Warrenton eagerly withdrew her original motion, as did Mr. Jenks his second. She then seconded Hopkins' proposal and stated her enthusiastic support. After what seemed to some an interminably long silence, the crucial swing vote came from Mr. Jenks — to the surprise of everyone except his granddaughter, who had extracted a near—promise of support from him the day before. As expected, Martindale was delighted to jump on the bandwagon. Dr. Jenkins, who had almost been forgotten in the excitement, indicated that he had no objections, and the motion then passed by a 4-1 vote, with Jim March dissenting.

Thus did non-punitive grading come to Midwest Community College. Who made the decision? Marvin Anderson, its sponsor, was possibly most responsible, but without the help of many others it would surely have died along the way. The opposition of the Faculty Senate and the dean of instruction might have killed it; the enthusiasm of the students probably deserves credit for rescuing it. But without the changes forced by its critics, it might well have been laughed out of town. Without the active support of interested citizens' groups, the Board of Trustees might not have dared to consider it. And the opposition of other community organizations helped force them to come up with a compromise policy that spoke to the concerns of all those with a stake in the future of MCC. And, perhaps the single most influential act of all was the behind-the-scenes lobbying of Mr. Jenks' granddaughter.

# CHAPTER 11
# Collective Bargaining

Much of what has been discussed so far may well be rendered obsolete by the phenomenon which is the topic of this chapter — collective bargaining. This phrase conjures up wildly differing visions in the minds of those interested in community colleges. Some picture teachers walking picket lines while students pound in vain on their classroom doors; others envision the college turning into a vast assembly line producing credits and degrees like automobiles; and still others see Libra bearing her scales of justice finally in balance between the administration and the faculty. Union members tend to think of collective bargaining for community college teachers as the extension of an inalienable right to a hitherto deprived group; consumer advocates fear it as yet another opportunity for employer and employee to reach mutual agreement at the expense of the public; and political scientists see it as a transfer of power from the lay citizenry to the professional staff. Collective bargaining can be, of course, all of these and none of these, depending on the time, the place, and the people involved.

### What is Collective Bargaining?

Most books and articles assume that the reader knows what is meant by "collective bargaining." This is not necessarily true. Although it is well understood in the worlds of business and industry, its meaning is often fuzzy to those whose lives have been spent in education. As a result, each observer is likely to give free rein to his or her imagination when contemplating the arrival of collective bargaining in a particular state or community college.

Many educators tend to look on collective bargaining simply as "a challenging way for an academic community to conduct an experiment in group dynamics."[1] The truth of the matter, however, is that collective bargaining refers to "a definite process shaped by history and defined by law. It is a specific means by which persons identified with a particular enterprise, separated into management and labor components, are enabled, in a highly formalistic way, to discuss certain issues that lie between them, to reach binding agreement on how to handle these issues, and then to be governed by that agreement in the work relationship for a fixed period."[2] The term "collective" derives from the fact that employees yield the right to negotiate individually with their employer and select an agent who bargains on behalf of all employees within a defined unit.

Collective bargaining became a leading system of controlling employer-employee relations in the American economy in 1935, when Congress passed the National Labor Relations Act. This Act, however, regulates only the private sector of the economy. The right to bargain collectively was subsequently extended to employees in the federal public service via governmental regulations. The right of state and local employees to bargain collectively is a function of state law, and by 1974 some 21 states had adopted statutes extending this right to teachers in public colleges.

When a state legalizes collective bargaining for its community college faculties, it *permits* but does not *compel* those covered to use this method of reaching agreement with their employers. Faculty members thus exercise this right at their own discretion. Nor do collective bargaining statutes dictate the terms of an agreement between employer or employee or even require that an agreement be reached. Although state laws vary widely, they generally impose on both parties the obligation to bargain collectively, in good faith, and at convenient times. Each side must be prepared to make genuine offers and counter offers, but neither side is required to agree to a proposal made by the other side or to make a concession. If an agreement is reached, the law may provide that either party may ask for a written contract to be executed.[3]

If, however, agreement cannot be reached, an "impasse" is declared to exist. The law does not require that an impasse be broken at the negotiating table. Any one of several post-impasse procedures, developed in the course of forty years of collective bargaining in business and industry and government, may be called into play at this time. They all involve the intervention of a third party with training and experience in helping parties to negotiations overcome their difficulties. These intervenors can be individuals or a committee, government officials or private specialists. They can be used as mediators, as fact-finders, or as arbitrators.

"Mediation" refers to the use of a neutral agent or third party to help the opposing sides work their own way out of the impasse. Mediators usually meet with the parties to the dispute in private to help find a solution, but they have no authority to make findings or rulings. "In mediation, the search is not for the correct or best or fairest solution, but for one that is acceptable to both sides."[4]

"Fact-finding" describes the formal process whereby a third party reviews the record, gathers new evidence if desired, and sometimes recommends a way out of the impasse based on the facts as he or she sees them. Such recommendations are usually not binding, but the attendant publicity can bring powerful pressure on both sides to accept them.

"Arbitration" involves turning the problem over to one or more impartial experts who are charged with finding the right way to resolve the issues. They hold hearings, gather evidence, and render rulings which are usually binding on both parties. Sometimes the parties involved are required by law to submit their dispute to arbitration; at other times they agree to do so on an *ad hoc* basis.

In the private sector, the ultimate weapons for settling disputes are strikes (by employees) and lockouts (by management). These methods are generally illegal in the public sector but are sometimes used nonetheless by government employees when an impasse is reached.

### Differences between Public and Private Collective Bargaining

There is some feeling that both strikes and binding arbitration take on a different coloration when utilized in the public sector. The strike's power to force agreement is based on the fact that it works economic hardship on both employer and employee. This same sanction may not exist for public community colleges. Although teachers do indeed lose salary while on strike, it may be that the employing institution will not suffer as much financial injury: state and local subventions may continue while expenses are reduced. Strikes at the elementary and secondary level are given added impact because closure means the withdrawal of child-care as well as educational services. This disrupts the lives of many citizens and generates intense pressure for settlement. This particular sanction, however, would not affect post-secondary institutions.[5]

Because of the limitations — both legal and practical — on the strike, other ways have been developed to increase bargaining strength in public enterprises. These include public relations campaigns, the lobbying of state and local officials, and direct political action at election times.

Binding arbitration — the other major technique for settling intractable disputes — also appears in a different light when applied to the community college. In industry, the matters submitted to an arbitrator have to do almost exclusively with wages, hours, and working conditions — personal concerns, so to speak, unrelated to the management of the enterprise except insofar as they affect its financial situation. In education, by contrast, the matters at issue are often of the greatest concern to the public at large, having to do with the educational program and the governance of the college. Submission of such matters to arbitration is tantamount to giving an outsider, with limited understanding of the peculiar needs of a community college and no legal responsibility to its constituents, the right to make decisions of the utmost importance to them. This means that their elected representatives, the trustees, are shorn of the power to make these decisions and therefore cannot be held accountable for them. The public thus loses the only way it now has of controlling a community college: through a governing board chosen at the polls or by officials who have themselves been elected.

The use of binding arbitration to settle community college disputes raises serious questions of sovereignty. Can a government yield its final authority to an outsider? Can trustees, who are vested by law with the authority to govern the campus, legally enter into a contract that abrogates some of this authority? Even after several years of debate, experience, and court decisions, these questions remain unanswered. The weight of judicial decision and legal opinion seems to be in the direction of accepting arbitration for determining questions of due process but rejecting it for deciding matters of substantive judgment. In other words, an arbitrator might force a board of trustees to accord due process to an employee it does not want to retain, but he could not make the decision as to whether or not the individual's qualifications are such as to merit retention. The whole thorny question of delegating power to a mediator can only be settled by the highest tribunal of each state or by the adoption by legislatures of precisely-worded statutes describing management rights and the scope of bargaining.[6]

### Scope of Bargaining

Another aspect of collective bargaining that is poorly understood in Academe is its scope. In the private sector, employees turn to collective bargaining in hopes of improving their terms of employment: wages, hours, and working conditions. There is little interest in changing the power structure of the enterprise for which they work.

Such is not the case in higher education. Although economic issues are undeniably important, matters of institutional governance often seem to be paramount. A recent publication of the California Teachers Association states that "The sole gain the faculty expects from a collective bargaining law is a legally guaranteed share in the governance process of their community college."[7] In contrast to industry, where employees are only periferally involved in managing the enterprise, community college teachers are deeply involved in making decisions about the operation of the institution and its educational program. Thus they tend to consider that such policy matters also fall within the scope of the collective bargaining process. The president of the California Federation of Teachers recently wrote that "The practitioner should be central to the decision-making process in public education. In that we are a profession, our scope of bargaining must not be limited to wages, hours, and working conditions."[8]

Faculty members in states with collective bargaining laws seem to be putting these tenets into practice. During the 1974-75 academic year, for example, several institutions of higher education were under threat of strike by their faculties. In some cases, wages alone were involved; in one, class size was also at stake; in another, wages and governance were both at issue; and in still another, the main dispute was over the faculty role in governance. Faculty members in Alaska struck over salaries, class size, and campus governance, while Nassau Community College teachers threatened to strike over the role of department chairmen and a proposal to give administrators first crack at vacancies on the faculty.[9] Perhaps the most striking example is in Massachusetts, where the statute authorizing collective bargaining by public employees has been interpreted as *excluding* salary issues from the negotiating process.

In response to the apparent lack of limitations on the scope of bargaining, school "managers" in several states are making a concerted effort to narrow it through legislation and collective action. The Institute for Responsive Education urges that, in order to protect significant student, parent, and community influence, it may be necessary to "limit sharply the scope of bargaining, keeping as many educationally significant issues and questions as possible off-limits."[10]

The laws authorizing collective bargaining often do include restrictions on the topics to be included in the negotiating process. Despite this, a recent study of trustees' and administrators' opinions on collective bargaining found that 68 percent of them considered its scope to be a source of controversy at their institutions.[11] One author sums up the difficulty of limiting the scope of bargaining as follows: "as a practical matter the scope of bargaining is influenced very little by statutory constraints. The dimensions of the process are in fact a function of the relative power of the two parties and the extent to which the members of the bargaining unit are ambitious to assert authority over and assume responsibility for decisions which bear on the management of the enterprise."[12]

## Extent of Collective Bargaining

The first states to grant collective bargaining rights to college faculties were Delaware and Michigan in 1965 and New York in 1967. By 1975 24 states had collective bargaining legislation of some kind covering higher education, and 20 others were considering it. Faculties at a few institutions had won collective bargaining rights without state legislation, although there is some doubt as to the legality of their contracts.

It has been estimated that, while in 1965 only 10,000 faculty members in higher education were under some form of collective bargaining, by 1972 almost 100,000 had this status. By the fall of 1975 some 224 community colleges had either certified bargaining agents or collective bargaining agreements in existence.[13] Those states with the largest number of faculty members covered are those who authorized it first: Michigan and New York. By contrast, a few states which authorized collective bargaining by college faculties had seen no use of it.

### Why Collective Bargaining in Higher Education?

Community college faculties have been attracted to collective bargaining for many reasons: some of these are common to all of higher education, others are peculiar to the community college. Foremost among the former is the tremendous expansion which took place during the 1960's: from 1959 to 1969, for example, total enrollment in degree credit courses nationwide rose from 3.4 to 7.3 million students.[14] As colleges grew, the locus of decision-making moved farther and farther away from the individual faculty member. As multi-campus institutions and multi-college systems emerged, the control centers moved away even from the individual institution. To direct this explosive growth, state agencies charged with controlling or coordinating all institutions of higher education proliferated. This imposed another layer of decision-making upon the local one, increasing still further the feelings of impotence experienced by those in the classroom. This feeling of frustration at losing control over their professional lives was accompanied by a growing sense of alienation, of loss of community, as the informality characteristic of small colleges was replaced by the impersonality of the multiversity. In response to these changes in the scale and structure of our system of higher education, faculty and other staff members began to seek new ways of participation in the governance process.

The last decade has also been a period of rising expectations for economic returns. Demands for greater compensation were brought on by the favorable professorial market and the spectacle of other professions improving their economic position. All studies of the factors leading to collective bargaining show that the expectation of economic gain ranks high on the list. By the early 1970's the enhancement of job security became a motivating force also: the threat of reduced enrollments, of the reduction of financial support, and of the oversupply of teachers encouraged college faculties to investigate labor union ways of protecting their positions.

The growing power of students in college governance has also made collective bargaining more enticing to some faculty members. Student demands for participation are often seen as a threat to faculty hegemony in those areas of decision-making traditionally reserved to them. Interestingly, students' initial reactions to the concept of faculty bargaining have been favorable; they see it as an opportunity for teachers to assert their claims against what is often seen as the common enemy: the administration and the board of trustees. Obviously, however, if the faculty expects to protect its domain from student intrusion via collective bargaining and students expect to enhance their control over their own academic experience, someone is doomed to disappointment. Since the areas of maximum student concern — the curriculum, the grading system, teaching methodology, and the like — are also those of maximum faculty autonomy, these two groups may eventually clash. Students may come to find that their interests are less well protected by the collective bargaining process in which they have no formal representation than by the legal governing agencies (boards of trustees) responsible to the body politic of which they are a part. The relationship of students to educational collective bargaining in some ways resembles that of the consumer to industrial negotiations: employer and employee may be so anxious to end the unpleasantness that they bargain away the rights of third parties who have a valid interest in the outcome of negotiations.

Groups of employees rarely enter into collective bargaining on a wholly spontaneous basis. Even if they are highly dissatisfied — and therefore presumably ripe for organizing — some external stimulus is usually required to prod them to action. This seems to be equally true of industrial workers and of college professors.

A positive effort to organize them — either by an outside agency or by a campus agency that is not part of the college's formal governance structure — is necessary. On campus this role is often played by faculty members acting for whatever organization seeks to become the faculty's bargaining agent. These in-house workers are in turn aided and abetted by agents sent out from local, state, or national headquarters of the labor or professional organization seeking a foothold on the campus.

The current wave of collective bargaining in higher education may thus be at least partly attributable to the special attention labor unions are currently giving to teachers at all levels. They look upon the organization of this profession as a foot-in-the-door to signing up other professional groups — engineers, physicians, social workers, lawyers, and nurses. These, along with other white collar workers, represent an untapped reservoir of potential union members almost equal to the present union membership. Albert Shanker, A.F.T. president, stated upon his election that: "Higher education is one of the great areas of organizing that is available to us . . . Organizing college professors will be a top priority of my administration."[15]

### Why Collective Bargaining in the Community Colleges?

"Collective bargaining in higher education found its earliest acceptance in the public two-year college. In June of 1972, 119 of the 158 separate institutions with recognized bargaining units served this sector of higher education."[16] Clearly, there are certain conditions peculiar to community colleges that make their faculties most susceptible to the allure of collective bargaining. One theory is that, as newcomers to the field of higher education, they are looked down upon by their supposed peers in four-year colleges and universities. No longer mere high school "teachers," not yet full-fledged college "professors," they are professionally insecure. Professor Lewis Mayhew calls them "marginal men," people who have left one reference group but have not yet been accepted into another. "Characteristics of marginal men are anxiety, punitiveness, rage, and a search for scapegoats. The administration is available and a union or a militant senate is a potential instrument."[17] This syndrome is not confined to community college faculty alone; instructors in former teachers' colleges which have been upgraded to comprehensive "state college" or "university" status exhibit similar insecurities. The consensus seems to be that "the professors most likely to support collective bargaining are those from less prestigious colleges, those with fewer scholarly achievements, those in the lower ranks, and the untenured and younger faculty members."[18] This is not to imply, however, that *only* teachers fitting this description favor collective bargaining: as early as 1969 a survey showed that "53% of the professors from top-rated colleges, 54% of those from universities, and 54% of those with tenure thought there was place on campus for faculty bargaining."[19] And, although in 1972 some 75% of those institutions of higher education with collective bargaining were community colleges, by 1975 their share of the total had dropped to less than 60%.[20]

Community college teachers may also be more comfortable with collective bargaining because many of them formerly taught in high schools where unionism is more professionally acceptable than in colleges and universities. "Managements are often said to have the labor relations systems they deserve. Thus, the elementary and secondary educational systems with characteristically authoritarian managerial styles have been fertile ground for collective bargaining."[21] And, as noted earlier, the governance structure of many community colleges is still closer to that of the high school than of the typical senior institution.

A recent study of the growth of collective bargaining in New Jersey found that high on the list of predisposing factors was "authoritarianism within the colleges' administration. This behavior, demonstrated through unilateral decision-making by administrators, was often characterized by the faculties as being arbitrary as well. In spite of committee structures and-or college senates or assemblies . . . the faculties believed they had little effective participation in governance."[22] Although not all community college faculties share this outlook, a considerable number apparently do. They have been disappointed to find that the assumption of the title of college professor does not automatically confer upon them all the prerogatives traditionally presumed to accompany it. Thus, while faculty in long-established senior institutions look upon collective bargaining as a means of *preserving* their traditional powers from attack by students and outside agencies, community college teachers see it as a means of *gaining* powers they do not yet have.

Finally, there is one other important reason for the sudden spurt in collective bargaining at the community college level: only recently has it become legal. Some observers credit the passage of enabling legislation with stimulating the spread of collective bargaining. One is tempted to ask, however, "Which came first, the chicken or the egg?" Are state legislatures moved to act on collective bargaining only when the demand for it is already great? Or does the passage of such legislation advertise its possibilities to previously disinterested faculties? The only sure thing is that a rash of collective bargaining agreements usually follows hard on the heels of their legalization. In New York state, for example, 90% of the faculties in well-established community colleges were actively organized within five years after collective bargaining became legal.[23]

### Impact of Collective Bargaining

Commenting on the recent spate of books on collective bargaining, Philip Semas opined that "A lot of the material simply isn't worth reading. Much of the rest is technical and of interest only to those actually involved in bargaining . . . Even more is repetitious: students of collective bargaining seem to be especially good at restating the little that is known about the subject."[24]

The fact of the matter is that it is still too new for anyone to be really sure what its long-range consequences will be. Not enough data has yet been collected to permit the drawing of scientifically valid conclusions. Thus, all that can be done at this point is to make some educated guesses, to point out its potential effects so that those embracing collective bargaining do so with their eyes open.

### Collegiality

Many faculty and administrators fear that collective bargaining will be the beginning of the end for collegiality, usually considered to be one of the distinctive characteristics of an institution of higher education. A major obstacle to assessing this is the fact that collegiality is, in the words of Ray Howe, "a term as loosely

defined as it is widely used."[25] To most people in higher
education it refers to the atmosphere of cooperation presumed
to exist among all those engaged in the operation of a college or
university. It implies a system of shared authority whereby some
decisions are made by faculty, others by administrators, and still
others jointly. Faculty have what amount to co-management
rights in many areas: courses of instruction, selection of colleagues, determination of grades and degree requirements,
academic freedom, and the like. On some campuses they have
virtually complete control over these matters, subject only to an
occasional veto by administrators or trustees. Faculty and administrators are considered to be professional equals, with each bringing
certain distinctive talents to the educational enterprise. When
conflicts occur, an attempt is made to resolve them by the
consensus process.

Collective bargaining, by contrast, assumes that faculty and
administrators are competitors rather than colleagues. It divides
them into two separate − if not necessarily hostile − camps:
management and labor. There is some question as to how faculty
committees and academic senates fit into this system. Whose side
are they on? Under the shared authority system, they make many
management-type decisions. What happens if some faculty
members are unhappy with scheduling decisions, for example,
made by the faculty senate? Normally, they would bargain over
such topics with management, but in this case they themselves
are management. In other words, as Pogo once discovered, "We
have met the enemy and they are us." A confusing situation, one
that industrial collective bargaining mechanisms may not be
capable of dealing with.

Inherent in the idea of "bargaining" is that each side must ask
for the moon in order to leave itself some maneuvering room.
Administrators accustomed to pleading with the board of trustees
for higher faculty salaries find that this is no longer permitted.
They may not even concede anything to those across the table
without receiving a comparable concession in return. The faculty
leadership, in turn, must convince its members that management
is being "extremely unfair, unreasonable, punitive, and even
vindictive"[26] in order to keep them from succumbing too quickly
to its offers. The negotiating process, thus, tends to drive faculty

and administrators apart, to stress their differences rather than their common interest in community college education. Persistent disagreements are settled by compromise, by finding a middle ground between the extreme demands of both sides, rather than by seeking a solution acceptable to both.

Other observers, however, feel that collegiality in the community college cannot be killed by collective bargaining because it has never really existed. Howe states that "the principal components of collegiality . . . are peer relationships coupled with mutual respect . . . While faculty and administrators do have some kind of relationship, it contains no semblance of true peerage."[27] True peerage, he predicts, is much more likely to come about with collective bargaining than without it, because participants in negotiations are equals in every sense of the word. He suspects that few truly controversial issues are really settled by consensus: what the administration calls "consensus" may well appear to the faculty to be "unilateral decisions." He questions whether there is any inherent reason why consensus should be preferred to compromise as a mechanism for reaching agreement on controversial topics. Although collective bargaining is seen by many as creating conflict, others see it as reducing conflict, since its fundamental purpose is to provide a means for solving problems.[28]

Proponents of collective bargaining in community colleges hope that they will be able to have the best of both possible worlds: they will get as much as possible via the carrot of collegiality, then turn to the stick of negotiations to get still more. Its opponents say, "No way — *either* we are colleagues working things out together in a cooperative way *or* we are adversaries fighting things out across the bargaining table."

A recent Carnegie Commission Report concludes that "There are several routes to power but they cannot all be followed simultaneously. The basic choice is between (1) codetermination and (2) collective bargaining or (3) some combination where the former is effective in some areas (curriculum) and the latter in others (salaries.) There is some question as to whether the latter is possible, since collective bargaining may have an irresistible tendency to move into all areas . . . It should be clearly understood that faculty members cannot have it both ways — they cannot engage in codetermination and in collective bargaining on the same issues at the same time."[29]

### Institutional Autonomy

Friend and foe alike fear that collective bargaining may tend to erode institutional autonomy. For one thing, the outside world is always present at the bargaining table: professional advisors are there from the state or national offices of the bargaining agent; negotiators are constantly aware of and influenced by settlements reached at other institutions; and the general policies of the union or professional organization representing the faculty influence their stance at the bargaining session.

As collective bargaining becomes widespread, there is a strong tendency for basic issues to become the topic of statewide negotiations with the governor and the legislature. In the final analysis, negotiators want to go where the money is, and, for most community colleges, it is at the state level.

A related possibility is that if their fellow citizens feel that local boards are giving away the store to the faculty, the state legislature will move in to set things to rights. As a result of pressure from dissatisfied constituents, it may pass even more detailed laws controlling faculty loads, use of travel funds, sabbatical leaves, and other aspects of the college operation which have traditionally been handled at the campus level.

Institutional autonomy is also diminished when a third party is called in to arbitrate between faculty and management. Whatever the decision, it is made by someone outside of the institution who may or may not have a thorough understanding of community colleges in general and local conditions in particular. If the shift to collective bargaining leads to an increase in the use of binding arbitration, the professional as well as the institutional independence of community colleges may be jeopardized.

Colleges have traditionally enjoyed greater freedom from public scrutiny than most other publicly-supported institutions. One reason for this is that their internal workings are somewhat mysterious to the average citizen. The disputes, grievance mechanisms, and impasse proceedings attendant on the collective bargaining process may well end all this: they make exciting newspaper headlines. There is concern that this publicity may bring about a loss of privacy, of prestige, and of public support. Others feel that this will be all for the good, that it will once and for all end the myth that education is too sacred to be exposed to the hurly-burly of everyday life.

## Written Contracts

The execution of written contracts to codify the agreements reached through collective bargaining may bring a hitherto unknown element of rigidity into the college governance process. A contract has a specific life span, and changes cannot easily be made during this period. Another byproduct of the written contract may be increased conformity: all departments and services on the campus will be required to do things in the same way. Community colleges, which have always prided themselves on their ability to "swing" with the changing needs of their communities, may find the written contract particularly confining.

Its proponents, on the other hand, look upon it as a much-needed protective device: since nothing can be altered without the concurrence of the bargaining agent, no unilateral changes can be made by management. The faculty role in governance, for example, is currently somewhat tenuous. Since it is based solely on authority delegated by trustees or administrators, it can theoretically be withdrawn or altered at their pleasure. Faculty need not even be consulted about – let alone agree to – this change in role. Such a unilateral action would not be possible under a collective bargaining contract, thus giving to faculty participation in governance the legal guarantee it now lacks.

## Expansion of Trustee Role

Some observers predict that the involvement of trustees in the day-to-day operation of the college will markedly increase where written contracts are in force. Trustees are assigned specific duties under the terms of many contracts and bear primary responsibility for seeing that they are carried out. This greater specificity of function may require them to devote considerably more time than heretofore to their trustee duties. Some welcome this as a return to the practice of earlier days when trustees were intimately involved in every aspect of school operation. If past experience is any indicator, however, administrators and teachers alike can be expected to deplore this trend. Ironically, while collective bargaining may force the board of trustees to give up some of its policy-making prerogatives to the faculty, it may force the latter to give up some of its cherished freedom in implementing these policies.

**A Decade's Experience**

Any assessment of the impact of collective bargaining on the community college at this time is bound to be highly speculative. This is particularly true in the area of governance: although changes in wages and fringe benefits can be readily documented, alterations in the power structure are much slower to emerge and more subtle to detect. Since bargaining has been permitted for a decade in several states, however, some results are beginning to come in. Attempts to evaluate them have so far been limited, but the conclusions of those studies available are worth noting.

One survey attempted to find out what the "managers" — administrators and trustees — think about collective bargaining. Information was gathered from representatives of 263 carefully chosen school districts — 53 community college and 210 elementary–secondary — in the 24 states where it was being practiced. There were no perceptible differences between the opinions of community college and public school participants, nor was there any relationship between the length of time (from one to nine years) collective bargaining had been in effect and its acceptability to the "managers."[30]

In a word, the respondents did not think much of collective bargaining. Only 6% thought its overall impact on their institution was good; 25% thought it was bad and the rest felt it had no effect. Although few of the questions dealt directly with the governance issue, forty-seven percent of the managers felt collective bargaining had weakened their rapport with faculty (6% thought it had improved it) and 62% reported more management problems than before (2% reported less.)[31] A study of trustees and administrators on 23 New York state campuses confirms this view: the majority felt that the effect of bargaining on campus governance and educational programs was more negative than positive. They did, however, identify as helpful outcomes the clarification of both faculty and management rights, the delineation of faculty duties, and the acceptance by faculty of greater responsibility for setting and enforcing professional standards.[32]

One hundred faculty members on these same New York campuses were queried as to their reaction to collective bargaining. They credited it with bringing about, in addition to higher salaries and fringe benefits, the following: a more important role for faculty in the governance process, increased communication between faculty and administration, and more sharing of responsibility for selecting administrators and supervisors. They described the new relationship as "governance by mutual consent."[33]

Students in several states have become sufficiently concerned about the effects of collective bargaining to seek the right to participate in the process. Student involvement has been permitted at three state colleges in Massachusetts, at Ferris State College in Michigan, and at Bloomfield College in New Jersey, while the Brooklyn Center of Long Island University allowed students to sit in as observers. The Massachusetts students felt that they had exerted considerable leverage, with both faculty and administration courting their support.

In 1975 Montana became the first state to give its students the right to participate in collective bargaining, as members of the public employer's team. This ground-breaking action was soon followed by legislation in Oregon which gave students an even larger role in the process: they now have access to all written documents, are able to comment at any time during the talks, and may meet and confer with both parties during the sessions. If this is a harbinger of things to come, students may well be destined to play a major role in collective bargaining in the community colleges.

Experience in the New York community colleges also confirms the expectation of external intrusion into what were formerly purely campus matters. The degree and type of interference, of course, will vary with the legal structure of each state. In New York, the counties are involved in community college financing, and through this door they have entered into the colleges' policy-making process. Under New York's collective bargaining laws, community college trustees often find it more convenient to step aside and let county officials negotiate directly with their faculties.Thus the allocation of resources — perhaps the most important activity of any governing board — passes to outside hands. Even more ominous is the fact that trustees have to consult extensively with county officials on a wide variety of policy matters. The latter may disapprove actions the trustees want to take on the grounds that they might preempt possible issues at the next round of bargaining. And "in several cases county officials have interfered with campus academic and cultural affairs by threatening retaliatory action in future negotiations and budgets."[34] At the administrative level their meddling is even more apparent: county executives often give orders directly to the community college president on certain political and economic matters.

There is also mounting evidence that state lawmakers will step in with regulatory legislation if they think that local faculties are winning too many concessions from their boards. Two cases in point are the recent efforts of legislatures in Michigan and Florida to regulate teacher loads in the community colleges of their states. And the New York experience tends to confirm the suspicion that "elected officials, once involved in campus affairs, find it too politically alluring to resist future temptations."[35]

## Conclusions

For many — if not most — community colleges, collective bargaining is either here today or coming tomorrow. Thus, all are avidly trying to peer into the future in an effort to predict its effect on their own campus. But since its history in higher education goes back barely a decade, the results to date do not provide a very reliable guide. So far, it seems that both the hopes and the fears of analysts of collective bargaining are being borne out. Teachers report satisfaction with the increased economic benefits they feel it has brought them. Trustees and administrators are disturbed by the increased discord and management problems they attribute to bargaining. All agree that it has brought about greater faculty participation in governance, but they may disagree as to whether this is boon or bane. Students are beginning to realize that they may have to seek seats at the bargaining table in order to protect their interests. And there is reason to believe that the feared outside interference by lawmakers and officials at both state and local levels may indeed materialize. Only more time, however, will tell if collective bargaining will drastically alter community college governance as we know it today.

## References

[1]Robert K. Carr and Daniel K. Van Eyck, *Collective Bargaining Comes to the Campus* Washington, D.C.: American Council on Education, 1975 p. 157.

[2]*Ibid.,* p. 157.

[3]*Ibid.,* p. 9.

[4]*Ibid.,* pp. 166-7.

[5]E.D. Duryea, Robert S. Risk, & Associates, *Faculty Unions and Collective Bargaining,* San Francisco: Jossey-Bass Publishers, 1973, p. 25.

[6]*Ibid.,* pp. 94-5.

[7]Community College Association — California Teachers Association, "Statement Prepared in Answer to Questions Submitted Last May by the Joint Legislative Committee on Postsecondary Education," p. 1, in letter to Ms. Zoglin dated November 27, 1974.

[8]Raoul Teilhet, "Collective Bargaining," *CALPHER Journal,* March/April 1974, p. 16.

[9]"Faculty Walkouts," in *Chronicle of Higher Education,* January 13, 1975, p. 2.

[10]Institute for Responsive Education Staff, "Collective Bargaining: Bringing Citizens to the Round Table," *Citizen Action in Education,* Vol. II, Number 1, Fall 1974, p. 5.

[11]Donald M. Ross, "A Survey of Collective Bargaining in Public Schools," made by the Personnel Committee, Community College Section of the California School Boards Association, Sept. 1973, p. 3.

[12]Duryea, *op. cit.,* p. 33.

[13]"Collective Bargaining on Campuses," in *Chronicle of Higher Education,* June 9, 1975, p. 5.

[14]Duryea, *op. cit.,* pp. 10-11.

[15]*Chronicle of Higher Education,* Sept. 23, p. 2.

[16]Duryea, *op. cit.,* p. 88.

[17]Lewis P. Mayhew in Clarence R. Hughes, Robert L. Underbrink, Charles C. Gordon, *Collective Negotiations in Higher Education, a Reader,* Carlinville, Ill,: Blackburn College Press, 1973, p. 51.

[18]*Chronicle of Higher Education,* Oct. 7, 1974,, p. 10

[19]*Ibid.,* p. 10.

[20]"Collective Bargaining on Campuses," *Chronicle of Higher Education,* June 9, 1975, p. 5.

[21]Duryea, *op. cit.,* p. 22.

[22]James P. Begin and Stephen Browne, "The Emergence of Faculty Bargaining in New Jersey," *Community and Junior College Journal,* Vol. 44:4, pp. 18-19.

[23]Duryea, *op. cit.,* p. 91.

[24]*Chronicle of Higher Education,* October 7, 1974, p. 10.

[25]R. Howe, *The Community College Board of Trustees and Negotiations with Faculty,* Washington, D.C.: American Association of Community and Junior Colleges and Association of Community College Trustees, 1973, p. 74.

[26]Ronald Campbell, "Collective Bargaining: Some Reflections of a President," *Community and Junior College Journal,* Vol. 44:4, p. 27.

[27]R. Howe, *op. cit.,* p. 74.

[28]*Ibid.,* p. 75.

[29]Carnegie Commission on Higher Education, *Governance of Higher Education: Six Priority Problems,* New York: McGraw-Hill Book Co., April 1973, p. 47.

[30]Donald M. Ross, *op. cit.,* p. 14.

[31]*Ibid.,* p. 3.

[32]Duryea, *op. cit.,* p. 100.

[33]*Ibid.,* p. 100.

[34]*Ibid.,* p. 102.

[35]*Ibid.,* p. 102.

# ✦
# CHAPTER 12
# The Future

Community college governance is undergoing major and rapid changes. The many reasons for this have been enumerated earlier and need not be repeated here. Suffice it to say that those interested in understanding the decision-making process must take into account these emerging trends as well as current conditions.

## Institutional Autonomy

One of the most widely deplored of these changes is the gradual but steady loss of campus independence. This is due partly to heightened activity at the state and national level and partly to the proliferation of multi-college systems.

State legislatures and executive offices pour forth a stream of statutes, edicts, and regulations designed to mold the community college to their vision of what it should be. Where there is a strong tradition of local autonomy, agencies are created to coordinate the colleges; in other places, state boards are given direct responsibility for establishing and operating community colleges. The result is that in more and more states the locus of decision-making is removed from the campus to the state capital.

The independence of individual community colleges is also threatened by the much sought-after federal funds. As Congress provides more and more dollars for higher education, it also doles out more and more restrictions and requirements. And collective bargaining brings onto each campus labor unions and professional organizations whose goals and policies are national in scope.

The loss of institutional autonomy at the local level is usually an unintended by-product of success: as the original college becomes overcrowded, it spawns a second or even a third or fourth sibling campus. To administer this growing family, a central organization has to be set up. Certain areas of decision-making then move from the campus to the central office. In terms of governance, these large multi-unit agglomerations — even if locally controlled — exhibit some of the same characteristics as state systems. The operative factors seem to be the size and number of colleges rather than the legal locus of control. Perhaps our lexicon of governance terms should be expanded to include the concept of "institutional" control. Community colleges could then be identified as operated in one of three ways: as part of a state system, as part of a local system, or individually by the community surrounding a single institution.

### Internal Struggles

While external forces eat away at their sphere of action, those within the college — administrators, faculty, and students — jockey for control of their diminishing domain. The greatest concentration of authority within the community college traditionally lay with the president and his chosen administrative staff. The current movement is to allocate some of these powers to faculty and students. The former tend to gain jurisdiction over curriculum, academic standards, and personnel policies — matters which professors in four-year institutions have traditionally controlled. Students, on the other hand, are wresting control of campus speakers, newspapers, bookstore operations, and student body funds from their staff advisors. Court-ordered extensions of freedom of speech and due process guarantees to the campus further enhance their independence from administrative and faculty domination. Students also are seeking a greater voice in classroom-related decisions; future conflicts may arise more with the faculty than with the administration.

### Intra-Segmental Conflict

The existence of stresses and strains within each segment makes it difficult to predict the course of governance within a given community college. Although the administrative group is usually small enough to present a united front, students and faculty are not. The latter is divided by age, by philosophy, and by discipline, while the former exhibit the entire range of characteristics typical of the adult population of the United States. Thus a high degree of intra– as well as inter–group rivalry may exist within a community college.

### Role of the Public

Perhaps the least known quantity in the governance equation is the general public. There are indications that this sleeping giant is about to awaken and assert control over public education at all levels. Scholarly journals debate the importance of lay control of the schools, newspapers and popular magazines increasingly carry articles on the topic, and citizens' groups are organizing to translate theory into practice.

There are also countervailing forces which may nullify this trend toward greater citizen involvement. The growing bureaucratization of the schools may stifle all attempts at participation. The transfer of power to state and national agencies may make it almost impossible for citizens to influence their community colleges. As the locus of decision-making moves farther and farther from the campus, the average citizen can no longer even identify the controlling office or agency, let alone hope to influence it. Frustration, apathy, and alienation result. Collective bargaining may turn out to be a mixed blessing in this respect. On the one hand, it may give greater publicity to the decision-making process and require greater trustee involvement in college operations. On the other, it may take away via the negotiating process some of the rights previously reserved to the lay public.

With or without collective bargaining, indications are that the voters expect their trustee representatives to play an ever more active role in determining the course of their community colleges. The inclusion of greater numbers of citizens in decision-making via advisory committes and participatory management techniques is on the rise. The extension of the vote to 18-year olds may mean the opening of a whole new era for the community colleges; students across the country are making their newfound strength felt in trustee elections and appointments.

Since this situation is unique to the community college, its long-range implications are unknown. Nowhere else in public education do consumers — actual and potential — have such a direct opportunity to decide what educational offerings will be made available to them.

### Conflicting Philosophies of Governance

It is clear that all the community college constituencies — both internal and external — do have a share in the decision-making process. The federal government and the courts provide the general framework within which the particular social institution known as the community college operates. Congress, through categorical aid grants and scholarships and loans, encourages colleges to offer programs it feels to be in the national interest to those students it feels deserve educational opportunities. Constitutionally, the states bear responsibility for the entire educational system, and their primacy in community college governance is undisputed. They decide when, where, and how public two-year colleges are founded and exercise varying degrees of control over their operation. The interest of all the people within the state in educating their citizens is thus protected. Local communities also have a say in this process: in some states it is a major one, with local boards of trustees endowed with broad decision-making powers; in others it is relatively minor, consisting only of advisory powers. Internally, the president and other administrators exercise many of the theoretical powers of the governing board, be it state or local. Much of their authority — for either legal, practical, or traditional reasons — is re-delegated to the teaching faculty. Students share in this process in two ways: they sit on decision-making committees and councils within the college and they influence the choice of trustees through their voting power.

That each affected group should have a voice in community college governance is not in dispute. *How much* power each constituency should have is very much in contention. A brief summary of the arguments put forth by each of the claimants may help to clarify these issues.

There are two basic philosophical differences among those competing for power in the community colleges. The first has to do with *who* should have the final authority, the professional staff or the lay citizenry; the second has to do with *where* this authority should be located, at the local or state (or even national) level.

## Lay vs. Professional Control

The case for the primacy of civil authority over the community colleges is based on the generally accepted democratic doctrine that "the social services crucial to the public's welfare and survival should be subject to the public's will. Schooling is no exception."[1] Professor William Cowley elaborated on this thesis as follows: "Why have institutions of higher education been established and by whom? The answer seems clearly to be, first, that they have been organized to disseminate and to advance socially beneficial knowledge, skills, and attitudes; and second, that civil governments have created them for the good of the general community. They have not been founded for the sole or even the primary benefit of professors, administrators, students, trustees, or all of them taken together, but, instead, for the benefit of society at large. Hence in all countries civil government, the most inclusive agency of society, retains the right to set them in motion and, further, to require that their governing boards represent the public interest."[2]

Others, however, feel that "professors should have final if not exclusive authority in academic government and that the public interest should either be unrepresented on governing boards or be so small as to be impotent."[3] Faculty, by virtue of their professional expertise, are seen as being in the best possible position to determine and to fill the educational needs of the general public. Those opposed to this concept reject it as syndicalistic, implying that every group of workers should manage its own affairs unchecked by the other interest groups and only vaguely by society as a whole. "The adoption of this political philosophy would mean that military civil servants would be unrestrained by the management of civil government."[4] On the lighter side, some doubt the ability of faculty to govern their institutions even if they were granted that right. One author states that "Colleges and universities are paradoxical in containing the greatest concentration of intelligence combined with the least capacity or inclination to apply it to collective governance."[5]

Sociologist Talcott Parsons, on the other hand, would assign to faculty a sort of fiduciary role; he concludes that "the responsibility of the academic man is . . . not primarily to a group of persons, but rather to the integrity of his devotion to the learning process in its many ramifications."[6] This is, in turn, refuted by Lewis Mayhew, who states that ". . . the special qualifications of faculty members to hold knowledge in trust has finally become suspect . . . faculties are not capable of assuming corporate responsibility . . . Institutions of higher education are social institutions created to serve the public need. A variety of forms of public scrutiny and demands for public accountability seem appropriate."[7]

Some of this dissonance may stem from the failure to distinguish between means and ends. One observer finds that "Much of the discussion about these matters tends to overlook the purpose of a college or university and views power as an end in itself. Some writers appear to assume that if only the dispossessed of the academic community (typically identified as the faculty, students, and staff) were at last endowed with power, there would be no further problems for the community, or, if there were, there would be no difficulty in resolving them. The ends to be served by the exercise of power are generally ignored in these writings."[8]

### State vs. Local Control

Assuming that there will always be some form of citizen control of community colleges, the question becomes one of finding the appropriate role for each *level* of government. The federal government, although usually considered too far from the scene of action to be effective, bases its claim to involvement on its legal and moral responsibility for the overall quality of life in the nation. An even more powerful persuader is its access to the pocketbooks of the taxpayers, which is considerably greater than that of any other level of government. Thus, it alone can play Lady Bountiful and, in return, can impose whatever conditions it wishes on the eager beneficiaries of its largesse. If the federal government chooses to enter the struggle for control of the community colleges in earnest, it will be a formidable contender.

The hottest controversy presently is over the proper relationship between state and local bodies in governing the community college. Should the state actually operate colleges or should it confine its role to assuring that they are provided by units of local government? The former is promoted in the name of efficiency, economy, and equality of financial backing. It is clearly simpler, from the state's point of view, to construct and to administer one system of community colleges than to work through cities, counties, or special districts. State systems, however, are almost inevitably perceived as characterized by rigidity, conformity, impersonality, and, in the long run, inefficiency. Local autonomy, on the other hand, is touted as conducive to experimentation, flexibility, diversity, and sensitivity to the needs of the populace. Regardless of the validity of these claims, most observers expect the balance to tip slowly but inexorably toward increased state control. In the event of a showdown, the state holds all the cards. Only a deep ideological commitment to local autonomy and a strong indication of support on the part of the electorate can prevent state lawmakers and officials from exercising their latent power over the community colleges.

Some feel that the key to the whole governance puzzle is the local board of trustees. In some ways a part of the college's internal governance system, in others a part of its external control system, it is strategically located at the confluence of all the competing interests. Perhaps it alone is in a position to establish "some kind of balance or equilibrium between the needs of the social system which supports the institution and the needs of the individuals within the institution."[9] Its strategic position, however, also makes it the natural target for all those wanting to enhance their role within the power structure. Federal and state legislators make inroads on the domain of the board from one side, while the professional staff closes in from another. It appears that if local governing boards are to serve as guardians of both lay and local control of the community colleges, they are going to need reinforcement. Those working toward this goal feel that

trustees must become more active and competent if they are to
ward off attacks from, on the one hand, increasingly militant
staff members and, on the other, increasingly active state
and federal officials.

## Conclusion

*The Final Carnegie Commission Report,* issued in 1973, finds
that it is not easy to determine who should govern higher education. The authors reject the concept of "consent of the governed,"
on the basis that educational institutions are not "governments"
with coercive power to enforce the law but rather "services"
which people choose to obtain or forego of their own free will.
Nor do they find the doctrine of "interest" to be of much help,
since almost everyone — students, faculty, administrators,
trustees, the public — has a different interest in the college. Nor
can a wise decision be made on the basis of "competence," which
they find to vary greatly among groups and individuals depending
upon the particular subject matter involved. Their final sum-
mation — which certainly applies to the community colleges
as well as to other segments of higher education — is as follows:
"The governance of higher education, we believe, is more a matter
of how good decisions can be made than it is one of any single
clear principle to be followed. We have concluded, generally,
that the structures of governance for higher education in the
United States are adequate as they now exist, with the need for
improvements rather than for basic reform."[10]
The final decision as to the proper way of governing our
community colleges will not, however, be made by a panel of
experts, no matter how capable and dedicated. It will, instead, be
made by legislators and officials in fifty state capitals, by trustees
in hundreds of board rooms, by students and teachers and administrators in thousands upon thousands of committee meetings, and
by millions of citizens in voting booths throughout the nation.
And this is as it must be, if the public two-year college is to remain
true to its mission as a *community* college.

## References

[1] James W. Guthrie, "Public Control of the Schools: Can We Get It Back?"

in *Public Affairs Report, Bulletin of the Institute of Governmental Studies,* University of California, Berkley, Vol. 15:3 (June, 1974), p. 1.

[2]W.H. Cowley, *op. cit.,* pp. 52-3.

[3]*Ibid.,* pp. 52-3.

[4]*Ibid.,* p. 54.

[5]Peter Barnett, "Authority and Purpose in College Governance," *College and University,* Vol. 43:3, pp. 159-67, p. 164.

[6]Talcott Parsons, "The Strange Case of Academic Organization," *Journal of Higher Education,* Vol. 42, pp. 486-95.

[7]Lewis Mayhew, in Talcott Persons, *op. cit.,* pp. 497-8.

[8]John D. Millett, *op. cit.,* p. 2.

[9]R.C. Richardson, Jr., *op. cit.,* p. 59.

[10]"The Final Carnegie Commission Report," *Chronicle of Higher Education,* Oct. 9, 1974, p. 14.

# Index